King Me

ACCEPTING A ROYAL INVITATION
TO A CO-WRITTEN LIFE

By John Voelz

Visit John Voelz at www.johnvoelz.com
www.facebook.com/johnvoelz
www.twitter.com/shameonyoko
www.westwinds.org
Visit Samizdat Creative's website at www.samizdatcreative.com

ISBN-100982612486
ISBN-139780982612484

Published in association with Westwinds Community Church, 1000 Robinson Road, Jackson, MI 49203
Published by Samizdat Creative, 5441 South Knox Court, Littleton, CO 80123.
All scriptures used in this Atlas are taken from the NIV translation unless otherwise indicated.

This book was written primarily for the people of Westwinds Community Church in Jackson, Michigan. It is part of a series of similar books called "Teaching Atlases," which supplement sermons and sermon series' during the weekend worship services. They are part study-guide, part reminder, part artifact.

Additional Atlases can be obtained through the office of Westwinds Community Church on a host of other topics.

If you would like to hire John for speaking or consultation, please email john@westwinds.org.

The set-up costs of each Atlas are privately donated by a Westwinds' parishioner, thus enabling extensive self-publishing at a reasonable cost. The proceeds from each Atlas are designated by the donor for a specific project—such as installing wells in developing countries, providing artistic and educational scholarships for children, or financially supporting pastors and missionaries around the world.

If you would like to donate to the Atlas project, please contact info@westwinds.org

Dedication and Thanks

For my directors and teachers. A psalm. For giving thanks. All in fun.

1   I will sing for joy to the people who invested in me;
        to you I am forever grateful.

2   To Charlotte who gave me my first Bible
        and expected I would love it.

3   To Ray who helped me see the Psalms like a puzzle;
        an adventure, a song, and a love letter.

4   To professor Needham who cried whenever he talked about
        The King, and made me cry as well.

5   To the musicians of Maranatha! Music who taught me to sing
        the Psalms, to memorize them, and to meditate on them.

6   To the people of Westwinds; I love to sing with you,
        to worship with you, to praise The King!

7   To Pastor George who played me my first Psalm set to music;
        and taught me to ask God to "consider my meditation."

8   To Aunt Jane who told me I was a poet
        and I believed her.

9   To Ken who told me I was a songwriter
        and I believed him.

10   I will sing for joy to the people who invested in me;
        to you I am forever grateful.

On The Design

This book makes use of QR Code technology.

A QR Code is a two-dimensional code that is readable by QR scanners, mobile phones with a camera, and smart phones.

If you have a smart phone, download any number of QR Reader applications from whatever source you get your applications.

When you scan the QR Codes in this book, your phone will direct you to a URL containing either video or text. Some are for further reading and information and some are just for plain fun.

I use the app QRReader on my iPhone that I downloaded from the iTunes app store. It works great. You may find one you like better.

Happy scanning.

Oh, and reading.

JVo

Table of Contents

Introduction

I was a kid when The King died on his throne. On August 16th, 1977, Elvis Presley died in his Graceland mansion. On the toilet. Well, on the floor. After he fell off the toilet. Not a very "kingly" way to go.

Much like the day President Kennedy was assassinated, or 9-11, or the day Michael Jackson died, many people remember what they were doing when they first heard the news.

August 16th was a Tuesday. I was home from school and playing outside when I heard my mom shout, "No!" I ran into the house to see who she was talking to. The T.V. was on. Mom was crying.

I instantly got it.

I started crying too.

It didn't matter that I wasn't really an Elvis fan. At 9-years-old I had already vowed my allegiance to The Beatles.

Everyone knows it is hard to be a sold out Elvis fan AND a sold out Beatles fan. I had to pick.

But I still got it.

Elvis meant something. Elvis changed things. Elvis was a way of life. An ideal. A metaphor for freedom. And tame rebellion.

When my dad got home, he put on Elvis records. Loud. He wasn't the only one. The whole neighborhood was listening to Elvis. My next-door neighbor played "Love Me Tender" over and over again.

I started listening to more Elvis from that day on. My grandma had some 8-Tracks of the Elvis gospel tunes. (True confession: I wasn't a huge fan of the gospel tunes.)

I liked the rock-and-roll Elvis. Let's face it, he had it all. Attitude. Looks. Movement. Girls. The voice. The guitar. Girls. The hair. Girls.

He grew on me.

I wanted to be Elvis. Maybe I still want to be.

Not the fat, bedazzled, Las Vegas Elvis. The 1956 Elvis.

But that's not happening. I did get the girl and I am very happy, but I look more like a lawn gnome than The King.

Elvis died when he was 42. My age as I write this. I am a little overweight. I have a toilet. I've been a little out of breath lately. Maybe I do have something in common with him.

The King is dead.

Kings die.

Kingdoms pass away.

They call him The King because he invented something. He made a mark.

He drew a line in the sand. He created a genre. Elvis was the first rock-and-roller. And that makes him rock-and-roll god. Little "g."

The fact that Elvis was first can be argued, but this is the gist of the origin of his name—The King of Rock and Roll.

Songs will forever be sung about The King. Stories will be told. Honor will be given.

But he's dead.

People still worship him, but he's dead.

You may have heard the speculation about Elvis being alive, but he's not. And he's getting tired of the jokes. I just had breakfast with him this morning and he told me he's had enough (ba-dum-bump).

The Book of Psalms contains a wonderful collection of songs known as the "Kingly Psalms." They pay honor to a king. "The" King. The King's name is Yahweh.

King Yahweh is alive.

It is King Yahweh I am referencing in the title, *King Me*.

"King Me" can be understood different ways depending on how we emphasize the words.

If we read it "King *Me*," with the emphasis on me, we might think this is a book about taking our rightful place in this world as the ruler of our own destiny. It is exactly the opposite of that.

If we read it with no emphasis on either word, we might conclude this is a book about a King and Me. The King and Me. This is a little closer to the truth.

If we read the title with the emphasis on the word "King," we might recall the instruction we give to our opponent in a game of checkers when one of our pieces makes it all the way across the board to their home row. In this case we say, "King me," and our opponent places another piece on top of our piece, allowing that double-stacked piece to move either forwards or backwards. This is even closer to what I am getting at.

The fact is, the title is a double-entendre. It has two meanings. It is a book about my life (your life) with a King and about how an alliance with that King allows us to experience abundant life—to have full range of the board.

Only by full engagement and submission to this King can we enjoy that kind of life. The King then becomes the co-writer of our story. We follow His lead and allow Him input.

That's what these Kingly Psalms (and this book) are about.

The writers of these Kingly Psalms unapologetically give honor to this king.

Psalms 47 and 93-100 make up this category of Kingly Psalms. Other spots in the Psalms mention The King, but the Kingly Psalms are specific to Yahweh's role as ruler over everything and His rightful place in the kingdom He resides over: the kingdom of the heavens, the earth, and the sea—and more importantly—a people.

Think of the Kingly Psalms this way:

Many people have written songs about rock-and-roll. The history of rock and roll. Memphis. Graceland. Many songs mention Elvis, The King. Just like all the Psalms (as a collection) make reference to and are about The King, Yahweh.

But the Kingly Psalms make reference to Yahweh the King in the same way Neil Young references Elvis in the song "He was the King":

> . . . The last time I saw Elvis
> He was singing a gospel song
> You could tell he had the feeling
> And the whole world sang along
> He was the King
>
> The last time I saw Elvis
> He was up on the silver screen
> Pushing a plough in a black and white movie
> And everybody started to scream
> Yes, he was the King . . .

("He was the King" by Neil Young)

Just as Neil Young celebrates Elvis, the Kingly Psalms celebrate Yahweh's deeds. His might. How He changed the course of history. They pay him very specific homage.

The Kingly Psalms inspire people with hope and encourage us in our faith. They give us a window to the past and a connection with our brothers and sisters of long ago. They are individual and they are corporate. They connect the worlds of the First and Second Testaments as we saw a people praising a King and longing for the Messiah—Jesus—who has revealed himself to us.

As a pastor who much of the time is consumed with studying, taking apart, analyzing, creating, writing, and sharing music, the Kingly Psalms catch my attention. They stick out among the book of Psalms—different structure, timbre, meter, rhythm, and tone.

This book you are reading is a musical journey. A poetic journey. It's a little bit of a history lesson. But more than anything, it's an invitation into the throne room of a King who has an invitation of His own to hand out.

An invitation to join in with others and celebrate.

An invitation to be edited.

To view your life through the lens of Kingdom life.

To become a self-fulfilling prophecy of a living song of hope.

To gain perspective.

To surrender.

King Me

Section One:

VEGAS AND THE IMPERSONATORS

Chapter One:

JAILHOUSE ROCK

Psalm 47

For the director of music. Of the Sons of Korah. A psalm.

[1] Clap your hands, all you nations;
  shout to God with cries of joy.

[2] How awesome is the LORD Most High,
  the great King over all the earth!

[3] He subdued nations under us,
  peoples under our feet.

[4] He chose our inheritance for us,
  the pride of Jacob, whom he loved.
  Selah

[5] God has ascended amid shouts of joy,
  the LORD amid the sounding of trumpets.

[6] Sing praises to God, sing praises;
  sing praises to our King, sing praises.

[7] For God is the King of all the earth;
  sing to him a psalm of praise.

[8] God reigns over the nations;
  God is seated on his holy throne.

[9] The nobles of the nations assemble
  as the people of the God of Abraham,
  for the kings of the earth belong to God;
  he is greatly exalted.

If the Kingly Psalms were a rock opera (and that's how I like to think of them), Psalm 47 would certainly do a good job of rocking the house from the start.

"Crank up the drums. Crank out the bass. Crank up my Les Paul in your face (a quote from Sammy Hagar's 'There's Only One Way to Rock.' It's a fun song even if it isn't true)."

Scholars have written many things about how to read the Psalms. We will discuss some of them here. Understanding form, genre, history, poetic device, setting, tone, word structure, original language . . . they can all be helpful in our study of the scriptures, and I think it is good to pursue all those avenues.

But while there are some very helpful scholarly tools to help us understand the Psalms, I like to start by asking,

"How does it make me feel?"

"How does this song move me?"

Honestly, this is how we approach any other piece of literature or art. We take it in, examining how it moves us. And good literature should move us.

Otherwise, we call it a textbook.

The Bible is not a textbook, just something we study. It is not simply a roadmap. It is full of poetry, song, romance, intrigue, murder, deception, history, prophecy, sex, love letters, wisdom . . . the list goes on.

So read Psalm 47. How does it make you feel?

There are nations clapping.

People shouting.

Cries of joy.

Celebration.

There has been a victory.

Promises have come true.

There is music.

The Tower of Power horn section is there.

People are singing.

Someone is shouting out instructions like a Jazzercise© instructor.

"Sing praises!"

Someone is pointing to a King.

It's a party.

It's chaotic.

It's *Jailhouse Rock.*

I've heard the Book of Psalms defined as an "instruction book" for us. Many books and devotionals have been written on how to "use" the Psalms to better your life.

Everything within me rejects that notion.

Maybe it's because I'm a feeler. Or a songwriter. Or a poet. They all blend together.

I can't read a Psalm like Psalm 47 and think of it as instruction manual.

It's an invitation.

It's a call to get on the Soul Train.

Could you imagine reading a book about "how to throw a party" and actually enjoying it?

1) Buy neato lights
2) Stock the fridge
3) Clean the house
4) Send out invitations
5) Plan some neato games

By reading that "how to" book, would you actually become a better partier?

The only way we can possibly view the book of Psalms as "instruction" is to place ourselves in the middle of the party and allow the psalmist to be our DJ.

If the psalmist is calling out dance moves, then sure, I can see it as instruction.

However, the instruction isn't like being prescribed medicine, it's instruction that comes by trying it on for size.

It's not step-by-step instruction.

It's instruction by immersion.

My wife is a great cook. In order to enjoy her food I simply have to open up my mouth and put the food inside. The experience is the lesson. If I don't try it, I don't enjoy it.

I need to experience her cooking in order to enjoy it. Reading her recipes, while she is a good writer, is not fun and it doesn't fill me up.

The instruction in the Psalms is that of accepting the invitation and experiencing God's goodness along with the blessing of unity with His people.

There is a scene that is played over and over in movies—it is a tried and true motion picture device. You can probably think of ten movies that use this same formula:

1. Somebody is depressed (usually over a guy or girl breakup).

2. The friends stand by, telling their friend to pull out of it and "cheer up" (usually with something like eating ice cream out of the carton together).

3. Then someone gets an idea to do something really crazy to

shake their friend out of this state of blah (a trip to Vegas usually works).

4. Next thing you know, they blow off work and pull an all-nighter celebrating and remembering what really matters—they have each other.

The empty talk and instruction to "pull out of it" never works. It takes breaking the routine and monotony, pulling together as friends to do something a little crazy, to move on and regain focus.

Maybe the Psalms are a little like a trip to Vegas (without the hangover or the regrets).

But only if we go.

Reading the brochure doesn't count.

Still, the Psalms are more than instruction. More than invitation.

They give permission.

To join in.

To shout.

To dance.

To laugh.

To cry.

There is a big "feeling" element to the Psalms.

My aunt Jane is a published poet and my uncle Bob is a painter. I spent a lot of time with them as I was growing up. Aunt Jane read me poetry and taught me how to write it. Uncle Bob gave me blank canvases, paint, and turpentine and coached me to make pictures. They also had a Kimball "Magic Chord" organ and a few songbooks they encouraged me to mess around with.

Auntie Jane and Uncle Bob encouraged me to perform as well—to share what I had created or learned. When family came over, they would ask me to stand on the coffee table and sing.

I remember very clearly performing Eagles' "Best of My Love" for all my cousins and their families. It was just part of who I was and who I was becoming.

It was natural.

Doesn't *everybody* sing and perform and paint and stuff?

Later in life, I found out the answer was "no." At least, not without encouragement, freedom, and permission.

Their encouragement and permission gave me the freedom I enjoy in worship today.

As I got older, I lived with that same reckless abandon and freedom of expression my auntie and uncle fostered in me. But . . .

The church tried to beat it out of me.

Not "The" Church, but the little church I was part of with my parents for awhile.

We sang while holding hymnals, starring straight ahead, not too much volume in our voices, definitely not making up any parts or straying from what the page said, cold, monotonous . . . I'm getting shivers thinking about it.

I so badly wanted to shake things up a bit. I asked if I could play guitar to liven the mood and use my talent for the church.

I was turned down.

Guitar was an instrument of decadence to these folks. Guitars drew attention to themselves, along with a host of other instruments.

There would be no guitar in The Sovereign Grace Reformed Baptist Church of Foresthill, California.

I wonder if they ever read the Psalms.

That was my experience.

So who beat you up?

Who or what tried to steal your joy?

What made or makes you scared to engage?

There is a great deal of freedom, encouragement and permission to participate in the Psalms. You don't have to look at the Psalms that are specifically music-centric (like Psalm 150) to see that celebration is part of the deal for the people of God. Even when instruments are not specifically mentioned (though implied since these are songs) there is a great rumble. Loudness.

Continuing with the "how it makes us feel" line of observation, let's ask some questions, looking more closely at what and who the people (and we by invitation) are celebrating.

Psalm 47 is grouped with 93-100 as a Kingly Psalm because of similar language, tone, and so on. But here, sandwiched in between 46 and 48, it makes great sense. 46 and 48 celebrate a kingdom, a city within a kingdom and a holy place.

This place is Zion—The Holy Mountain.

This place has a King.

This King is victorious.

Over all kings and kingdoms.

(We'll talk more about Zion in Chapter 8.)

Commentators point out that this imagery of a mountain, a city, and a king is metaphorical language very similar to the language used to describe the myths of the Canaanite pantheon of gods, whose chief deity was named El. In their mythology, El had a palace on a mountain, and all good things flowed from there.

The Hebrew poets may have borrowed this imagery to one-up the myths. Psalm 47 invites all nations and peoples to examine Yahweh, the great King, who rules over all.

But it's not just an "our God can beat up your god" sentiment, though there is a bit of that in the Psalms. It is an invitation. It is what some might call *evangelistic* in nature. It is headline news: *Extra! Extra! Read all about it! Yahweh is King. Come join the party.*

Some believe this song was commissioned and composed for use in the Hebrew temple corporate worship liturgy in connection with the Feast of Tabernacles (Sukkot). It was at one of these celebrations that King Solomon dedicated the temple in I Kings 8.

Imagine the scene. All the elders of Israel were called together along with the heads of the tribes, the priests, and the families.

Thousands were there when The Ark of the Covenant was brought into the temple.

It was like one of those college frat parties where word leaks out and the next thing you hear is someone saying, "How in the world did this happen?" Where did all these cars come from?

Except, in this case, no one said, "My dad is gonna kill me."

Dad was pleased.

God's presence showed up like a cloud and filled the temple.

King Solomon blessed the people and prayed. He reminded them of God's promises and what He brought them through and gave a passionate speech about the ultimate King, Yahweh.

He reminded the people that it was not about them.

     The temple could not contain God.

     The foreigner was welcome.

They partied for fourteen days straight.

I love the very center of the Psalm—verses 5 and 6:

     God has ascended amid shouts of joy,
     The Lord amid the sounding of trumpets.
     Sing praises to God.
     Sing praises.

Sing praises to our King.
Sing praises.

The "centers" of Psalms are important (we'll talk more about this in chapter 2). They are like the bridge, the part you are supposed to get. They are the summary. They drive it home.

In Elvis's rendition of "I Can't Help Falling in Love with You," I have always loved the bridge:

Like a river flows surely to the sea
Darling so it goes
Some things are meant to be

The rest of the song is important. The other lyrics matter. They fill it out. They set the tone. But here, the melody breaks into a haunting minor key that stands out and grabs your attention. If you get nothing else, know that "I Can't Help . . ." is a song about fate. Love happens. Just like water flows downhill into the sea.

And so it is with the center of Psalms like 47. If you get nothing else, in case you are wondering what this song is about . . .

Yahweh is King.

There is a party.

You are invited.

Sing. Sing. Sing. Sing.

We will see similar sentiments throughout the Kingly Psalms.

So, how does Psalm 47 make ME feel? I feel like dancing. I feel like rocking. I'm bringing my guitar. I have been invited and given permission to raise the roof. Everyone is dancing.

Chapter Two:

MY WAY

This is not a book about biblical interpretation *per se*, but it would be a good idea for us to take a few moments to talk about the rules of engagement when it comes to the Psalms. We'll keep it simple. There are things to look for and understand that will help us in our interpretation, enjoyment, and participation in these oldies but goodies.

When my son was young, I remember him asking me if I have ever listened to a song that made me cry but I didn't know why.

I have.

I still do.

We are supposed to feel emotion in songs.

Especially songs about life, humanity, God, the human condition . . .

God made us that way.

We are emotional creatures.

But, He also made us something else—He gave us more than emotion.

He gave us intellect.

If all we ever did was sit around in circles and ask how the Bible makes us feel, we would come up with some crazy interpretations of scripture.

And some do.

But I can't just read the Bible "My Way."

I believe the Bible is saying something, though not necessarily just one thing. Not that each specific verse only communicates one specific truth—I believe in layers of meaning. Scripture is deep and multifaceted.

What I am saying is—it doesn't just mean "anything."

We can't make up stuff about the Bible because of what we think it is saying to us based on an emotional reaction.

There are rules to interpretation.

The words of the ancient Psalms, these lyrics, this Hebrew pop, contain meaning. And not just any meaning—sometimes they have many meanings, but not whatever we want them to mean.

There is a great story in John 4 where Jesus is talking to a woman about worship. He says (paraphrasing) that God is looking for worshippers who worship in spirit and in truth.

Spirit—

We worship with everything inside of us,

>   not only with our minds, but with our whole being.

>   We respond to God from that place within us that is
>   indefinable and involves our very soul.

Truth—

Our minds are engaged,

    we understand,

        we fully realize,

            we ponder,

                we gain intelligence,

                    and are not ignorant.

                        We genuinely respond
because of what we know to
be true.

Even when we don't *feel* like worshipping God, we can worship based on the *truth*.

All these things are going on in the Psalms. There is emotion and partying and celebration and a big hoopla, and there is some good, sound, solid theology.

We know God more because of the Psalms.

We know more *about* God because of the Psalms.

To pull out the truth, the theology, the "what is being said" of any section of the Bible, we need to know a few things.

First, we need to know WHAT we are reading. This is often referred to as "genre."

If you go online to Netflix to rent a movie (since all video stores are going bankrupt) and you are looking for the movie, *There Will Be Blood*, you will look in the drama section of the website. You won't go to the comedy section. You won't search under documentaries. And it won't be listed with the T.V. shows.

Those are the wrong genres.

You know the gist of the movie already and you have a certain set of expectations for it. It is a motion picture drama. If you approach *There Will Be Blood* as a comedy, you will be sorely disappointed, maybe angry, or frustrated that it didn't deliver. But the movie is not designed to make you laugh.

The Bible is the same way.

The Psalms are a particular genre of scripture.

C.S. Lewis points out:

> Psalms are poems, and poems intended to be sung; not doctrinal
> treatises, nor even sermons . . . Most emphatically the Psalms
> must be read as poems; as lyrics, with all the licenses and also
> the formalities, the hyperboles, the emotional rather than logical
> connections, which are proper to lyric poetry.

C.S. Lewis, *Reflections on the Psalms*

In October of 1938, a radio adaptation of Orson Wells' classic *War of the Worlds* was broadcast in New York City.

People gathered around the radio in their homes to listen that night, as was their custom. But on this particular evening some people missed the intro to the program—had they listened, they would have known what was going on.

The dramatic program ensued with the passion of an intense radio broadcast bringing news of great gloom and doom. The "reporter" was talking about an invasion happening "right now."

Some were new to this kind of radio fantasy and were a bit confused. Some were caught up in the anxiety and tension inherent in news broadcasts in the days leading up to World War II. Many didn't know how to interpret the genre.

Whatever the case, history tells us a couple million people believed the science fiction broadcast was actually taking place and Martians were invading NYC. Another million or so reported being "genuinely frightened and concerned," and a few others probably didn't want to admit that they soiled themselves as well.

It was a radio program. A fantasy. Had they known the rules, had they known how to engage it, the outcome would have been different.

So it is with the Psalms.

We need to know the point. It will make our reading and study that much more accurate and fulfilling.

Ray Lubeck, in his book *Read the Bible for a Change*, retells the account of former Green Bay Packers coach Vince Lombardi and a famous locker room speech he gave on the first day of football practice in 1965.

Lombardi stood in the midst of his players and held up a football. He looked them in the eyes intensely and said, "Gentlemen, this is a football." He was trying to make a point. They needed to get back to basics.

The point of the game of football is to move that ball down the field. It happens a bunch of different ways—it's tossed, launched, kicked, heaved, and sometimes bounced.

All the rules, strategies, and game plans get down to one thing.

The ball.

Learning to handle it.

Becoming comfortable with it.

Knowing how to use it—and not use it.

Lubeck uses this analogy to introduce a very good point—the Bible is a book. Yes, we believe it is God's Word, which elevates it to another level for us as Christ followers. But at the same time—not to devalue it in any way, but rather to help us value and understand it even more—we need to understand it is a *book*.

Not only is the Bible a book, it is a book containing many books. Those books were written by many different authors, each having his or her own style, personality, figures of speech, tone, and organization.

The authors were all writing with unity in their purpose and with the same system of faith and history to draw from, yet they were all distinctly different. What is fascinating, however, is that scholars—those from the church world and secular theologians as well—marvel at the cohesion, the unity, the clarity, and the consistency of a text written over centuries of time.

Even the time that separated the authors makes the writing unique because of the distinct cultural and historical settings in which they were writing.

Within my parents' first few years of marriage, my dad (being a good husband and remembering his anniversary) went to the store to buy my mom an anniversary card.

He hurried home, proud of himself that he hadn't forgotten, and presented my mom with flowers and a card. My mom was overcome with joy at his thoughtfulness and romantic gesture.

Until she opened the envelope.

The front of the card my dad had painstakingly picked out for my mom for this momentous Hallmark moment read:

"To a Fine Priest."

Now, had my dad done it as a joke, it may have been funny. There arc rules for jokes. This would have fit within that framework.

Unfortunately, it was *not* a joke—even though it has become one now at my father's expense.

The writer of that card intended something COMPLETELY different for what it represented, to whom it was to be presented, and how it should be understood. The words on the card didn't change, but the message suddenly became ALL WRONG.

Because dad wasn't careful.

After we know *what genre* we are reading, we need to identify the *authorial style*. Hallmark cards have a style. Those who write Hallmark cards have a style.

The Apostle Paul writes differently than Moses, who writes differently than Solomon, who writes differently than John, who writes differently than the writers of the Psalms.

This is a good thing. Once we understand an author's writing, we can better understand what he is saying. This also makes for much better reading.

We don't want Steven King writing romance novels.

Those who shape the stories flavor the intent.

If I use the book of Song of Solomon as a recipe for romantic love with my wife, she is either going to be severely disappointed, or angry, or both. The first time I refer to her "twin gazelles," it's over. That is not what the author intended.

When we read and study the Psalms, we are students of poetry.

T.S. Eliot once said,

> Poetry is not a turning loose of emotion, but an escape from
> emotion; it is not the expression of personality, but an escape from
> personality. But, of course, only those who have personality and
> emotions know what it means to want to escape from these things."

T.S. Eliot, "Tradition and the Individual Talent"

In a humorous way, Eliot suggests poetry is not for casual reading or the casual heart.

Of course, you would expect a poet to say that.

So what are some things we need to look for in the Psalms? What are the rules of poetry? How does Hebrew poetry differ from Dr. Seuss? How are the authors using this genre to say what they want to say?

Poetry, or poetic language, is a major deal in the Bible. About a third of our Bible contains poetic language. The authors use poetry to say a lot in a few words, tugs on the heart strings, make it memorable, and stretch us to think in new ways.

The Book of Psalms is a fascinating collection of poetry. The Kingly Psalms are a genre within a genre. These poems are well crafted by men and women for use in worship. They are songs about God (The King in 47; 93-100), to God, by God's people.

Below are some things to look for in biblical poetry that you can refer back to as you study the Kingly Psalms, and any psalm for that matter (*all the questions and examples in this next section are from Ray Lubeck of Multnomah Bible College and Seminary, y and are used with his permission, and are not to be reprinted*).

<u>Things to Look for in Biblical Poetry</u>

Question: What is poetry?
Poetry is a form of writing where normal language is changed to intensify its impact. Poetry is a "kind of language that says more and says it more intensely than does ordinary language" (taken from *Sound and Sense: An Introduction to Poetry* by Laurence Perrine).

Question: What are some ways this is done in English?

Often English poetry uses rhyme or rhythm (meter):

> Roses are red
> Violets are blue
> Sugar is sweet
> And so are you

Poetry also "bends" the normal rules of grammar, punctuation, and word order.

> Out of the fertile ground he caused to grow
> All trees of noblest kind for sight, smell, taste;
> And all amid them stood the Tree of Life,
> High eminent, blooming ambrosial fruit
> Of vegetable gold; and next to life,
> Our death, the Tree of Knowledge, grew fast by—
> Knowledge of good, bought dear by knowing ill.

John Milton, *Paradise Lost*

Question: How is it usually done in biblical poetry?

The key feature of biblical poetry is parallelism. Parallelism is the "rhyming" of thoughts and forms rather than sounds.

The grave	*cannot*	*praise you*
Death	*cannot*	*sing your praise.*

Isaiah 38:18

There are several kinds of biblical parallelism:

Synonymous: The thought of the 1st line is repeated in the second.

Yahweh is my light and my salvation	*whom*	*shall I fear?*
Yahweh is the stronghold of my life	*of whom*	*shall I be afraid?*

Psalm 27:1

I will sing	*to Yahweh*	*all my life*
I will sing praise	*to my God*	*as long as I live*

Psalm 104:33

Antithetic: The 2nd line states the opposite of the 1st line.

The prospect	*of the righteous*	*is joy*
But the hopes	*of the wicked*	*come to nothing*

Proverbs 10:28

Yahweh	*tears down*	*the proud man's*	*house*
But He	*keeps*	*the widow's*	*boundaries intact*

Proverbs 15:25

Inverted: The parts in the 2nd line are in reverse order from the 1st.

O Yahweh, | *do not forsake me*
Be not far from me, | *O my God*

Psalm 38:21

Synthetic: The 2nd line simply builds on the idea of the first.

You broaden the path beneath me
So that my ankles do not turn.

Psalm 18:36

(For more on Things to Look for in Biblical Poetry please see the NOTES section at the end of this book. It is well worth your time)

Beyond to clever poetry in the Psalms there is a deeper magic. The Psalms aren't "just" poetry and they aren't simply art or inspirational sentiment.

The Psalms are part of the canon of scripture. Part of our Bible. Part of God's word to us.

They are the words of *men and women* to God . . .

. . . and the words of *God* to men and women.

Don't step on my mind. It just got blown.

The Psalms give us a special peek into the spiritual life, practices, beliefs, mission, methodologies, and prayers of our ancient brothers and sisters who longed for a Messiah.

The promises and longings they sought after and sang about have become our songs. As Christians, we are sharers in a promise that the ancient Hebrews sang about, and we see the promise on the other side.

The Psalms tie us to our past and help us identify with our brothers and sisters from over 2500 years ago.

But they are also God's songs back to us.

Chapter Three:

LOVE ME TENDER

You don't need to Google "king" to spit out many examples of people who have had the title attached to them. Some we only call kings because of their greatness at doing what they do. Beyond Elvis, we might immediately think of The King of Pop, Michael Jackson; LeBron James (who goes by King James); or the Kings of Leon.

Beyond those kinds of kings, however, most of our ideas about kings and kingdoms come from the movies, followed by a few things we pick up on CNN—at least for those of us who live in the U.S.

We know of King Aragorn mostly because we saw the *Lord of the Rings* movies or read the books. We've seen King Richard depicted in a handful of movies—in one thousand of which he is connected to Robin Hood (hyperbole). And we've seen Richard Gere play a horrible King David.

Throughout history some kings came into power over a region through violence and the usurping of authority over a people and all their resources. Those kings then controlled the land and released resources back to the people, who paid them homage, taxes, and forced respect.

Kings, then, are born into power, take power, or are elected into power. Kingship usualllyusually lasts for a lifetime or until the king abdicates his throne.

The monarchy of Israel had an unusual inception. King Saul was the first king over all the tribes of Israel but he wasn't born into it, he didn't take it by force, and he wasn't really elected.

In I Samuel 8 the Bible tells us Israel wanted a king even though Yahweh wanted them to view *Him* as their king—they kept whining and Yahweh gave in.

The establishment of a monarchy in Israel was permitted by Yahweh because they has rejected Him repeatedly. Samuel anointed Saul king of Israel and presented him as Yahweh's choice for them.

Many of the kings in the Bible, including Saul, have gone down in history as men defined by their intoxication with power rather than their allegiance to Yahweh.

One glaring exception throughout scripture is the example of King David, whom Yahweh God described as a "man after His own heart" (I Samuel 13:14; Acts 13:22). The people loved David. He has gone down in history as a good king. He was imperfect and full of warts, but a good king who sought after God.

And, by the way, he was a songwriter and poet who penned many of the Psalms.

The King of the Kingly Psalms however, is a different kind of King.

He was not elected,

He did not steal power,

He was not born in to it,

He did not inherit a kingdom.

As a matter of fact, we might say

a people were born

and inherited a King.

King Yahweh is King because He birthed creation, a people, and the nations.

This King prefers to gain respect by stretching out His hands and saying, "look what I've done."

This King invites us into a relationship and dialogue in the Psalms.

He is unlike any other King. You are free to approach Him. He leans forward on His throne to hear what you are saying.

We learn a lot about the character of King Yahweh throughout the Psalms. With that being said, why is it some seldom look at the Psalms as books to "learn" anything from? Why do the Psalms usually end up as cuttings on the front of greeting cards?
It may have something to do with the structure and tone. Many of us are accustomed to associating poetry with casual reading and literature designed to cleverly inspire.

Oftentimes, because of the structure and tone of the Psalms, they are neglected as books that churches "preach" out of. They are used sparingly, read in between worship songs, or end up printed in the church bulletin.

But the Psalms are in every way, shape, and form the word of God and as such fit into the framework for scripture referenced in 2nd Timothy, which says

All scripture is God-breathed and is useful for teaching, rebuking, correcting, and training in righteousness, so that the man of God may be thoroughly equipped for every good work.

2nd Timothy 3:16-17

We've already discussed the fact that poetry and Psalms and songs are not simply instruction but rather invitation. We've discussed the fact that the Psalms are participatory.

The Psalms are also a conversation with the King.

You have been invited into the royal court.

You are the audience, and you have an audience.

God wants to say something to you, and He is waiting to hear from you.

How then is God speaking back to us through the Psalms that we originally spoke to Him?

Let's answer that question by zeroing in on the Kingly Psalms.

One of the main features of the kingly Psalms is they are full of "asking" *prayers*.

Prayers.

Petition.

Cries for help.

We need these prayer examples because sometimes we wonder how much we can ask of God. Not only that, we wonder how honest we can be in the asking. We get to be the proverbial fly on the wall as we read the prayers in the Psalms.

It's like watching an older sibling. My brothers had it made. I'm the oldest so everything I did broke new ground with my parents. I was the first to date, to cut school, to drive, to get a job. All they had to do was watch me to see what to do and what not to do.

They could also see my parents' reactions to everything I did wrong, gauging how merciful and graceful my parents were in situations that required grace and mercy.

In some ways, the Kingly Psalms allow us that kind of insight. We get to watch how the people wrestled with God and asked tough questions and how God responded. God said, "This kind of interaction is okay."

> O Lord, the God who avenges,
> O God who avenges, shine forth.
> Rise up, O Judge of the Earth;
> pay back the proud what they deserve.
> How long will the wicked O Lord,
> how long will the wicked be jubilant?
> They pour out arrogant words;
> all the evildoers are full of boasting.
> They crush Your people, O Lord;
> they oppress Your inheritance.
> They slay the widow and the alien;
> they murder the fatherless.

They say "The Lord does not see;
the God of Jacob pays no heed."

Psalm 94:1-7

This Psalm starts with a prayer that is also a discussion or
conversation. It is also a *complaint.*
If we were to rewrite this prayer as a paraphrase, we might write it
something like this:

Dear God,

We know You are King, and, as such, You are the Judge. We know
you have the power, but we are a little confused. A few of us here
have been talking, and we are a little fed up. I mean, how long is
this really going to go on? There are jerks running around yapping
their mouths and beating their chests like Tarzan all day long as
they trample on us. They aren't kind. They hate you. They hurt us.
They take advantage of us. This country is going to hell. No one
even cares about the hurting, the homeless, the kids who have no
place to go. Do You not see what is going on here?

Signed,

Jolted in Jackson

But the psalmist does something interesting next.

He answers his own questions . . .

. . . based on what he knows about Yahweh. He is crying out, naming his fears and trying to gain some perspective.

His answer is God's answer.

> Take heed you senseless ones among the people;
> You fools, when will you become wise?
> Does He who implanted the ear not hear?
> Does He who formed the eye not see?
> Does He who disciplines nations not punish?
> Does He who teaches man lack knowledge?
> The Lord knows the thoughts of man;
> He knows that they are futile.

Psalm 94:8-11

God is a bit sarcastic, but He's willing to talk it out.

This is how prayer works.

And, in most cases, this kind of interaction gives the psalmist and us great perspective. Towards the end of the psalm, the songwriter says:

> But the Lord has become my fortress, and my God the rock, in whom I take refuge.

Psalm 94:22

With prayer in the Kingly Psalms, there is a cry and a complaint, followed by perspective, and followed by praise.

It's not hard to recognize how the band U2 has been influenced in their songwriting by the Book of Psalms. Just look at some of the lyrics to their song "Sunday Bloody Sunday."

> I can't believe the news today
> Oh, I can't close my eyes and make it go away
> How long?
> How long must we sing this song? . . .
>
> ' Broken bottles under children's feet
> Bodies strewn across a dead end street . . .
>
> . . . There's many lost but tell me who has won
> The trench is dug within our hearts
> And mothers, children, brothers, sisters torn apart . . .
>
> . . . But tonight, we can be as one . . .
>
> Wipe the tears from your eyes, wipe your tears away . . .
>
> . . . The real battle just begun
> To claim the victory Jesus won

It's U2's prayer. It sounds strangely familiar, almost like someone has been reading his Bible and learning how to pray. Hmmm.

The Kingly Psalms give us a good model for prayer.

They also give us a good model for what is commonly known as *praise*.

When I think of praise, I think of the little game we played with all of our kids as they were growing up and still play to some extent. The game is called, "I Caught You Doing Something Good." We don't play it with them as much as we play it with ourselves as parents.

It's a discipline for us.
It's easy to get caught in a negativity trap. Like most of us, I am very good at finding fault with things.

Your room isn't clean.

Your chores aren't done.

You're lazy.

You didn't take the dogs out to potty.

The government is messed up. (I know that has nothing to do with my kids, but it is easy to jumble all our gripes together sometimes).

"Praise" is more of a discipline. With our children, I try to tell them daily at least three or four things they are doing well, things that value them, speak of their worth, and call out their special gifting.

I'm proud of you.

You are very talented.

You have great ideas.

You are creative.

You are the best daughter and young mommy I could ever imagine.

And so it is with praising Yahweh. It's a discipline wherein we take note of the things He has done and we call them out.

We say, "God, I caught You doing something good."

Psalm 93 gives us a good model for this kind of praise.

Just for fun, let's look at its layout based on what we learned in the last chapter (*see more on Biblical poetry in the NOTES at the end of this book*).

| The Lord reigns, | | He is robed in majesty; |
| the Lord is robed in majesty | | and is armed with strength. |

| The world | is firmly established; | it cannot be moved. |
| Your throne | was established long ago; | You are from all eternity |

The seas	have lifted up,	O Lord,	
the seas	have lifted up	---	their voice;
the seas	have lifted up	---	their pounding waves;

| Mightier | than the thunder | of the great waters, |
| mightier | than the breakers | of the sea-- |

the Lord on high is mighty.

| Your statutes | stand firm; | --- |
| holiness | adorns | Your house |

for endless days, O Lord.

Along with a ton of fun poetic devices, this psalm has a good example and invitation for praise. By the way, you might be able to arrange this poem differently. That is not the point. The point is there IS a structure. There is a message. The structure of this message is steeped in praise.

The psalmist orders this song so that the praise due Yahweh is juxtaposed to the praise that might be due the mighty earth. But The King, Yahweh, is mightier than all of it.

The earth, having been here for quite some time, is a force to be reckoned with.

But Yahweh established His throne from eternity.

The seas are lifting up a loud noise, like thunder. They are, in effect, praising. They are trophies of the One who put them there. Hear the sound? It's frenzied. It's in unison with creation. It's deafening, strong, and powerful.

But it's not ALL powerful.

We might also look at this Psalm arranged as a *chiasm* where similar thoughts are placed in mirror-image order. This particular *chiasm* is like a song that starts with a chorus, goes to verse one, then verse two, then the chorus again (*see NOTES at the end of this book*). A possible structure might be:

      A   Yahweh is a majestic and glorious King over all (v1a-b)
            B   Yahweh is King over the earth (v1c-2)
            B   Yahweh is King over the seas (v3-4)
      A   Yahweh is a majestic and glorious (and holy) King in Jerusalem (v5)

In the repetition and word pictures, we see an example of praise.

Look at the words and images that repeat and build upon one another.

Sound.

Strength.

Eternity.

The world.

His house.

Like any good praise song, the great images pull us deeper. So ask questions of the psalm. *Why? How? What does this image say?*

Scratch and sniff the images.

Verse one says He is "robed in majesty" twice. It also combines His reign with His strength.

Ask yourself why. Who dresses up in this world? What does power and might look like?

Think of the artist Prince. Have you seen what he wears? He wears clothes fit for monarchy. He doesn't call himself Prince for no reason. The dress matches the title, self-imposed as it may be.

This Person in Psalm 93 is a person in charge. Adorned. Everything is under Him. The psalmist uses military language.

This is a King you don't mess with (as opposed to the effeminate Prince, whom I'm pretty sure I can beat up, even though I love his music).

Instead . . . You praise Him for all that He is.

    Not what He stole,

        not what He inherited,

            but who He is and what He has done.

We praise Him because He shares that wealth with us. He invites us into His house. He's been there forever, and nothing shakes Him.

King Yahweh is a God who is good to His people. He hears their cries. He is patient. He keeps His promises. He loves his kingdom.

These things demand praise.

Section Two:

ELVIS HAS LEFT THE BUILDING

Chapter Four:

ALL SHOOK UP

In Chapter One we started by reading Psalm 47, the first in our grouping of Kingly Psalms. Go to the beginning of Chapter One or open your Bible and read Psalm 47 again. The whole thing.

Does anything stand out to you as something we have not yet talked about? I told you the Psalm makes me want to dance. We discussed the grandeur and majesty and power of this great King.

But we haven't talked about the twelve short words that precede verse one:

For the director of music. Of the Sons of Korah. A psalm.

At Westwinds Church, we put the words to songs on a screen so that everyone can follow along with the worship leaders. By law, we have to add some copyright information, authorship information, and a registration number that allows us to use each song.

In order for any church, bar, concert hall, or other establishment to legally use someone else's songs, certain steps must be followed every time that song is printed, recorded, broadcast/streamed on the web, or put on screen.

You may have noticed these bits of information on the screen if you come to Westwinds. They usually appear at the end of the song. By law, we can also put them at the beginning, but the end seems less distracting for a formality.

However, at times we have put the author information at the beginning, particularly if we are introducing a new song that was written by me or one of our other writers at Westwinds. (I like to play a game and leave my info off sometimes, to see if people will like the song even if they don't know I wrote it. I just told you a guarded secret. Now you know).

Song copyright information and other music facts are also present inside most music albums.

Along with the basic info required by law so everyone knows whom the songs belong to and whom to pay, there is a bit of information often referred to as "liner notes."

Liner notes, contrary to basic copyright info, are not a formality. They are there to give you more information about the song, the artist, and any other people or circumstance that added to the recording.

I love reading liner notes.

Oftentimes, when reading liner notes I have "ah-ha" experiences.

> "I *knew* that guitar solo sounded familiar. It was played by so-and-so who played on such-and-such's album!"

> "Oh, wow, I didn't know so-and-so wrote this song. That means a lot, especially because of what he is going through right now."

> "This producer always uses this same formula in the orchestration."

> "No way! She played on this album? I thought they were bitter enemies!"

Maybe you don't care as much as I do, and I would understand if you didn't.

Maybe you know exactly what I mean, and you can't wait to open the CD and read the liner notes as you listen, so you can get the full picture.

Most often, the notes like those at the beginning of this psalm and many others are regarded as the "necessary copyright info." However, scholars suggest we look at these notes differently. I would like to suggest we look at them as liner notes.

I say this because someone thought it was important to include them. These notes existed before copyright law. This addition isn't a legality. It's a message.

This brings up a whole set of questions regarding this first Kingly Psalm.

Who is the director?

Who is Korah?

Who are his sons?

What is a psalm? Aren't they all p psalms?

Scholars refer to this bit of liner notes as the "superscription" of the psalm. Like liner notes, superscriptions can tell us about an author, who the song was intended for, or what event the song is connected to.

In some ways, the superscription works much like the spot in liner notes where the band talks about the specific instrumentation they chose for the song.

In this particular case we have a psalm being designated as a . . . psalm.

Seems redundant. But as this designation is most often associated with "praise" songs in scripture, many scholars have come to believe that the designation of *psalm*—the actual word being *mizmor*—means it is supposed to be played with instruments and maybe a choir. It's big.

More scholarly circles (Nerd alert! Nerd alert!) show concern (maybe too much) over the preposition "of" in the psalm superscriptions. This same preposition can be translated "to," "concerning," "associated with," or "dedicated to." Yes, they mean different things. But I don't believe the translation is super important to the *meaning* of the Psalm.

Let me explain. If I write a song "to" my wife and you hear me perform it, you might say, "That is a gorgeous song. She is lucky to have him as a husband. He is a sensitive man. I bet this made her cry" (just go with me on this). If I write it "for" or "about" my wife, you will probably have the same reaction.

It doesn't matter if I dedicate it to her at the microphone or not. If I wrote the song for our anniversary, the song meaning is still the same and you may have the same reaction. If I wrote it concerning something that happened when we were dating long ago, the song remains the same.

What matters is the content, the story, the people involved. The meaning.

If I put that song out on an album, I will probably include the dedication to her or the reference that it is about her. This will help give you the context. If you know anything about me or my wife, the song will mean more to you by nature of our relationship to you.

If, for some reason, someone else writes the song about me and my wife, you can still view the song content through the lens of what you know about us.

All this to say, don't get too hung up on the *to, for*, or *of* of a superscription, but pause and ask what you know about the people who are involved to give you more insight into the context of the song.

So who is Korah?

First, let me start by saying his name means "baldness," so he must be special.

I know this because . . . I'm bald. Insert laughter here.

The First Testament has a few references to Korah. You can read about him in Exodus 6, Numbers 16, Numbers 26, and I Chronicles 6, to name a few. He lived at the same time as Moses and comes from the priestly line of Levi.

Korah had some issues. Things didn't turn out well for him.

In Numbers 16, Korah and a few of his buddies decided they didn't quite like the way Moses was handling things. They served the Lord in the duties of the tabernacle, but they wanted more. They wanted to be priests. They wanted the high office, to be regarded as something more special than they were (which was already pretty special). They didn't think it was fair that some people in their line got to be priests and others did not. Boo hoo.

They didn't set up a nice meeting with Moses and Aaron to talk about it. Think of it more as a scene out of *Beauty and the Beast* where the town folk gather together with pitchforks to "kill the beast."

Addressing these leaders and men of prominence, Moses told them to back down. He was very angry that they had challenged him, tried to bully him, and ultimately were angry with God.

Moses tried to talk it out with a few of the dissenters, but they refused to talk to him, accusing him of leading them into the wilderness to die. Apparently they had forgotten about the prison and hard labor they were forced to do in Egypt.

Moses suggested the men take it up with God. He told Korah and the 250 others, along with Aaron, to light their censers with incense and stand at the door of the Tent of Meeting to let God sort out who was priestly material.

As angry as Moses was, I don't think he knew exactly what was going to happen.

The Bible tells us that when the men gathered, "the glory of the Lord appeared to the entire assembly." What happened next was a scene out of a Spielberg movie.

> The Lord said to Moses and Aaron, "Separate yourselves from this assembly so I can put an end to them at once." But Moses and Aaron fell facedown and cried out, "O God, God of the spirits of all mankind, will you be angry with the entire assembly when only one man sins?"

> Numbers 16:20-22

Apparently, God saw things differently than Moses and Aaron did. This was not the sin of one man that needed to be dealt with, but the spirit of entitlement of an entire group of dissenters, including the guys who refused to talk it out with Moses earlier, even though they didn't show up to this particular meeting.

> Then the Lord said to Moses, "Say to the assembly, 'Move away from the tents of Korah, Dathan, and Abiram.'" Moses got up and went to Dathan and Abiram and the elders of Israel followed him.

> He warned the assembly, "Move back from the tents of these wicked men! Do not touch anything belonging to them, or you will be swept away because of all their sins." So they moved away from the tents of Korah, Dathan, and Abiram. Dathan and Abiram had come out and were standing with their wives, children, and little ones at the entrances to their tents.

> Then Moses said, "This is how you will know that the Lord has sent me to do all these things and that it was not my idea: If these men die a natural death and experience only what usually happens to men, then the Lord has not sent me. But if the Lord brings about something totally new, and the earth opens up its mouth and swallows them, with everything that belongs to them, and they go down alive into the grave, then you will know that these men have treated the Lord with contempt."

> As soon as he finished saying all this, the ground under them split apart and the earth opened its mouth and swallowed them, with their households and all Korah's men and all their possessions.

> Numbers 16:23-32

The story goes on from there. It only gets worse. Bottom line: the Lord doesn't smile upon the power-hungry whose motivation is to gain some kind of religious authority. He is not happy at all.

There is but one King. There is but one ultimate Power.

All of the ne'er-do-wells and malcontents who approached Moses and were ultimately killed took a position that "the whole community is holy" (Numbers 16:3). They were more concerned with their rights of power than with recognizing who held ultimate authority.

Numbers 26 tells us that this rebellion was ultimately a rebellion "against the Lord" (v. 9).

Even though many men rebelled against God, Korah was marked as the leader of the rebellion, and his name went down in history.

Numbers 26 says this lesson was to serve "as a warning sign." For them. For us.

Chapter 26 also says something we should take note of:

"The line of Korah, however, did not die out."

This is a mindblower.

The Bible does not specifically say that Korah died that day. His followers certainly did. But we can safely assume that Korah lived. And he lived with what he had done for the rest of his life. He saw the affect of his sin. He, his sons, and their sons lived on.

This Korah and these sons are who we read about in the superscription of Psalm 47.

Read the Psalm again.

Clap your hands.

The Lord is awesome.

Be joyful.

He rules over all.

No one is more powerful.

Join the rest of the assembly.

He is King over all the earth.

He reigns.

Alone.

Everyone is gathering to honor Him.

The kings of the earth belong to Him. He is exalted. He. Is.

Knowing what you know now, does Psalm 47 have a bit of a different flavor? Do you have a new perspective?

We also learn a bit more about the Sons of Korah from the Bible if we continue to dig a bit.

I Chronicles 6 includes a list of men that King David put in charge of the temple music. They are ministers of music who work in the temple.

This list is a large musical family. Think of them as the Family VonTrap on steroids. Please do not think of them as the Osmonds. Polyester bellbottoms would not have been allowed in the house of the Lord.

In this long list of names, we see a familiar one. Korah. One of his sons is listed here, as well as the sons after him. The Sons of Korah.

We know this is the same Korah because of the tribal linkage—the Kohathites. The head of this group of family musicians was Heman (not to be confused with He-Man and the Masters of the Universe). Heman was a descendant of Korah and the writer of Psalm 88. When you have some time, read that psalm with your new insider information.

The Sons of Korah were musicians and songwriters. Psalm writers. The Kingly Psalm 47 is not only about a powerful King, it is about a gracious King, a King who rewarded and looked highly upon the sons of one who betrayed Him.

That is something to sing about.

Chapter Five:

A LITTLE LESS CONVERSATION

O Lord, the God who avenges,

O God who avenges, shine forth.

Rise up, O Judge of the Earth;

pay back the proud what they deserve.

How long will the wicked, O Lord,

how long will the wicked be jubilant?

They pour out arrogant words;

all the evildoers are full of boasting.

They crush Your people, O Lord;

they oppress Your inheritance.

They slay the widow and the alien;

they murder the fatherless.

They say, "The Lord does not see;

the God of Jacob pays no heed."

Take heed, you senseless ones among the people;

You fools, when will you become wise?

Does He who implanted the ear not hear?

Does He who formed the eye not see?

Does He who disciplines nations not punish?

Does He who teaches man lack knowledge?

The Lord knows the thoughts of man;

He knows that they are futile.

Blessed is the man You discipline, O Lord;

the man You teach from Your law;

You grant him relief from days of trouble,

till a pit is dug for the wicked.

For the Lord will not reject His people;

He will never forsake His inheritance.

Judgment will again be founded on righteousness,

and all the upright in heart will follow it.

Who will rise up for me against the wicked?

Who will take a stand for me against the evildoers?
Unless the Lord had given me help,
I would soon have dwelt in the silence of death.
When I said, "My foot is slipping,"
Your love, O Lord, supported me.
When anxiety was great within me,
Your consolation brought joy to my soul.
Can a corrupt throne be allied with You—
one that brings on misery by its decrees?
They band together against the righteous
and condemn the innocent to death.
But the Lord has become my fortress,
and my God the rock in whom I take refuge.
He will repay them for their sins
and destroy them for their wickedness;
The Lord our God will destroy them.

Psalm 94

Can you think of a band that might be able to pull off a song like this and make it work? I have to be honest: all the bands that come to my mind at first are 80's Metal bands like Iron Maiden and DIO.

I can hear the whining of the guitars and the vibrato of a tenor voice singing.

The video would have dragons and wildebeests.

Parents would not allow their children to own the album because of the content and the cover art.

In Showtime's hit show *Dexter*, the audience follows the many escapades of a guy who studies the patterns of blood spray at murder scenes, only to hunt down and kill the people who inflict such pain on others. He helps police solve crimes and then takes justice into his own hands.

Let's be honest, a serial killer who kills serial killers is a brilliant idea. We may not admit it, but Dexter's "Dark Knight" persona is appealing. He takes care of what the system doesn't take care of.

We sometimes just want God to be our Rodney King in the sky, asking why everybody can't just get along. We want teddy bear hugs from Him when it comes to our own injustices.

But when the defenseless are taken advantage of, when children suffer, when people wield their power at the expense of other people, a nation, or a village, we want Dexter God.

If we are honest, we want Dexter God to show up for many less important and less intense injustices. We want God to bash in the teeth of our creditors who call late at night, our teachers who give us bad grades, and our girlfriends and boyfriends who left us for no apparent reason.

We're pretty vengeful.

At first blush, the God of Psalm 94 can appear to be vengeful in the same way as Dexter—a God who pays back, a God who wants people to "get theirs," and a God who might even enjoy the payback.

But that's not Him.

In John Calvin's commentary on the Psalms, he points out a more well-rounded and accurate understanding of the vengeance of God. He admits that while vengeance is never a happy word, it isn't haphazard. It isn't spiteful. It isn't just an "excitement of angry passions" or a lashing out.

Instead, we need to move away from Dexter God and think more of God's vengeance in light of a judge who works within a system of justice and righteousness, upholding those things to the very end.

Is it possible for any of us to celebrate justice with a pure heart? Can we celebrate the unjust getting their just reward? Can we feel okay about someone enjoying the natural consequences of his own horrid choices?

I think we can.

As bearers of the image of God, we have within us a sense of justice, of setting things right and working within a system.

One of my favorite movies is *Life is Beautiful*. If you haven't seen it, I am going to blow the ending for you in the next few paragraphs, but it won't blow any secrets *per se*—just a bit of the element of surprise and a satisfying denouement.

Life is Beautiful is the first subtitled movie I ever watched all the way through and forgot it was subtitled. I was enraptured by it the first time I saw it and have been many times since then.

The movie starts out in the years leading up to WWII in Italy, where we meet Guido, a hilarious Italian Jewish bookkeeper who courts and marries a beautiful woman and has a son with her.

The father and son end up in a concentration camp after the occupation of Italy by Nazi forces. Guido helps his son survive by telling him they are playing a game and they can earn points or have points taken away. They must be careful not to be disqualified. Guido tells his son that the grand prize at the end of the game is a tank.

At the end (and here's the big spoiler I warned you about), the liberation forces show up and Guido's son is lifted into the arms of an American soldier on a tank.

He has won.

Justice has prevailed.

The innocent child was spared.

But you know who didn't win? The Nazis.

And because of the hell they put people through and the hundreds of thousands who didn't survive, we are right in wanting justice.

Through the whole movie we are hoping and praying that little boy is not harmed and that there is liberation. And justice.

I have stood inside of a holding cell in the concentration camp at Auschwitz, Poland. I have put my fingers into the gouges in the walls of the cells where a priest used his fingernails to etch artwork into the concrete as he waited to die. I have seen the rooms full of human hair and luggage and shoes and eye glasses.

When I see these things, I pray for justice.

I want things to be right.

To be corrected.

I appreciate the honesty of Psalm 94. The Jewish people were surrounded by nations and peoples who assaulted, oppressed, killed, and tortured them. The psalmist is not crying out against just a general evil.

It is personal.

And the psalmist isn't just crying for someone to come beat up the school bully. He is crying for the Judge of the Earth. The big Judge.

What seems to make the psalmist even angrier and more conflicted is the fact that these evildoers are smug. They are giving God the finger. They think they are getting away with something.

And, for the time being, it sure looks like they are.

Verse four says they "pour out arrogant words." This Hebrew verb is also translated in other parts of scripture as "celebrate," "gush," and "bubble." They are spewing, boiling, spitting arrogant claims that they are somehow better than God and that they will prevail.

We've already seen what happens to people who make those kinds of claims and have that sense of entitlement. "Paging Korah, Korah, white courtesy phone, Korah."

Finally, it's important to point out the psalmist is not trying to assemble an army in verses 16-19.

> Who will rise up for me against the wicked . . .
> . . . take a stand for me . . .
> Unless the Lord had given me help,
> I would soon have dwelt in the silence of death.
> When I said, "My foot is slipping,"
> Your love, O Lord, supported me.
> When anxiety was great within me,
> Your consolation brought joy to my soul

Rather, the psalmist is acknowledging that God is his only help. Who will take a stand? No one can. Not the kind of stand that needs to be taken. Only God can take that stand. And it is a stand that brings peace.

The King is the Judge of appeals.

The songwriter is asking this King to "rise up" and "shine forth." He uses the same kind of poetic language we would use to describe the sun that shines light into the dark places. It is also the kind of language we use to describe the arrayment and presentation of a King.

This language reminds us of what we read earlier in Psalm 93 about the King being "robed in majesty."

Some have even suggested the "seas" in Psalm 93 are a metaphor for the nations—the same nations that the psalmist cries out against in Psalm 94.

The loud, crashing, chaotic seas list up "their voice" in 93 much like the people "pour out arrogant words" in 94.

As loud and as chaotic as they are, they will not ultimately win. We know the end of the story. They can flex their muscles and scream all they want.

No one can rule besides this King.

No other throne belongs here.

This King is the King of Peace.

He is just.

He will see his people through.

He will see that evil has its reward.

Chapter Six:

CRYING IN THE CHAPEL

You saw me crying in the chapel
The tears I shed were tears of joy
I know the meaning of contentment
Now I am happy with the Lord . . .

"Crying in the Chapel" performed by Elvis

Come, let us sing for joy to the Lord;
Let us shout aloud to the rock of our salvation.
Let us come before Him with thanksgiving
and extol Him with music and song.
For the Lord is a great God,
the great King above all gods.
In His hand are the depths of the earth,
and the mountain peaks belong to Him.
The sea is His, for He made it,
and His hands formed the dry land.
Come, let us bow down in worship,
let us kneel before the Lord our Maker;
for He is our God
and we are the people of His pasture,
the flock under His care.
Today, if you hear His voice,
do not harden your hearts as you did at Meribah,
as you did that day at Massah in the desert,
where your fathers tested and tried me,
though they had seen what I did.
For forty years I was angry with that generation;
I said, "They are a people whose hearts go astray,
and they have not known my ways."

So I declared on oath in my anger,
"They shall never enter my rest."

Psalm 95

One of the first praise songs I learned as a child was taken from this psalm. The song, taken from verses six and seven, was often referred to as "Come Let us Worship and Bow Down." My church often sang it as a call to worship—a song we'd sing at the very beginning of church services.

To be quite honest, I never knew I had memorized scripture by learning this song. I thought it was just a song a dude wrote that had a semi-decent melody and wasn't as horrible as the other songs we sometimes sang that made no sense to me.

But one day I learned that this song was actually called Psalm 95.

When I learned it was an actual psalm, like, from the Bible, I was stoked. I actually had memorized scripture without even knowing it (Just as an aside, I use the same trickery now as a church band leader. I love including scripture in songs or singing whole parts of scripture without anyone knowing it. Muwahahahahahahaha!).

I originally thought it was the whole psalm when I saw it printed out as "Psalm 95" in my camp songbook. I looked it up in my Bible to make sure.

I felt kinda ripped off.

It wasn't all of Psalm 95, but just a part.

And the next part got weird.

I quickly understood why we only sang one snippet of the psalm as I tried humming the same melody while singing, "Do not harden your hearts as you did at Meribah, as you did that day at Massah." Not only did the melody not work with the next part of the song, but the song didn't make sense anymore.

Isn't this a call to worship? Isn't this a happy song? I thought, "Did someone screw this up? Is this actually the *same* song?"

It felt so abrupt to me,

 this interruption.

It was like someone singing, "I Want to Hold Your Hand" and stopping to read a history book in the middle. What gives?

Why does the psalmist invite us to worship, bow down, sing, shout, and have a big celebration only to change the tone completely with warnings about some past rebellion, hardened hearts, and making God angry?

It *is* an interruption.

And that is how it's supposed to feel.

This change in tone is meant to grab our attention, to shift gears.

Now, all of a sudden it gets interesting. Why the interruption? What is so important that the song can't keep going as is? Who is interrupting?

At a glance, it seems like the psalmist is interrupting *himself.*

But he has a co-writer.

This is a Lennon/McCartney team.

Someone else has a voice.

I tried to think of some good examples of a song with two voices, but every one I came up with was cheese. Elton John and Kiki Dee's "Don't Go Breaking My Heart" is a tragedy, and "Run Joey Run" is perhaps the worst song in all of history, behind "We Built This City on Rock and Roll."

I digress.

Maybe it is better to think of this song, not in terms of pop music, but in terms of choral arrangements, musicals, or better yet, rock operas.

Being the careful Bible students that we are, we might want to grab a pen, some paper, a concordance, our Bibles (duh), and maybe access to the internet. One of the first things we might want to do is see if this passage or any part of it shows up anywhere else in scripture.

This is where the magic happens.

The Book of Hebrews is about the absolute, unmistakable, supreme power of Jesus: the High Priest, the mediator of the new covenant, the promise of the prophecies and the prophets. Throughout the book, Jesus is compared to others, such as the Father, the angels, Moses, and the priests.

Chapter three of Hebrews gives special attention to Moses.

What do we find in the middle of this chapter? We find Psalm 95:7-11 (which also happens to match up with the verse references of Hebrews 3—"7-11"—but that is just a coincidence, as strange and awesome as it is). It is an exact quote of the interruption section, the back half of the Psalm.

But there is one addition.

We see who the co-writer is.

The passage in Hebrews begins,

"So, as the *Holy Spirit* says . . ."

The Holy Spirit!

We also learn something else.

Hebrews chapter three is all about Jesus. Whenever we see words like "so" or "therefore," we should stop and ask what it is referring to. My Sunday school teacher always said, "When you see a 'therefore,' stop and ask what it is 'there for.'"

"*So*, as the Holy Spirit says . . ." is a phrase flowing out of the stream of thought that Jesus is superior to all. He is God.

And what does the Spirit say?

"Today, if you hear HIS voice . . ."

The second part of Psalm 95 is not only an interruption in thought. It is the voice of the Holy Spirit prophesying. The Holy Spirit is reminding the children of Israel of something that happened in the past and pointing them to the future.

Which begs the question, "What happened at Meribah and Massah?"

Another rebellion.

You can read about this rebellion in Exodus 17.

In this rebellion, the people once again were upset at Moses. There was no water. They were thirsty. But it wasn't their thirst that was wrong or bothersome. Anyone can understand that.

It was their attitude.

> Moses replied, "Why do you quarrel with me? Why do you put the Lord to the test?" But the people were thirsty for water there, and they grumbled against Moses.
>
> They said, "Why did you bring us up out of Egypt to make us and our children and livestock die of thirst?"
>
> Exodus 17:2b-3

They forgot where they came from.

> They forgot about God's provision.

> They were short-sighted and angry.

> This was not the first

> or the last time.

> Then Moses cried out to the Lord, "What am I to do with these people? They are almost ready to stone me."

The Lord answered Moses, "Walk on ahead of these people. Take with you some of the elders of Israel and take in your hand the staff with which you struck the Nile and go. I will stand there before you by the rock at Horeb. Strike the rock, and water will come out of it for the people to drink."

So Moses did this in the sight of the elders of Israel. And he called the place Massah and Meribah because the Israelites quarreled and because they tested the Lord saying, "Is the Lord among us or not?"

Exodus 17:4-7

According to commentaries, Massah means "testing" and Meribah means "contending." Not that we ever do that (wink).

We know from the book of Exodus the children of Israel had been freed from a prison existence in Egypt by the hand of Yahweh. They rejoiced in their freedom yet they were quick to forget about their deliverance as soon as Pain and Suffering Version 2.0 came along. They were quick to praise when everything was going well and quick to turn on Yahweh when things were less than comfortable.

In Psalm 95, they needed an interruption in their religious routine of song and dance. They needed a reminder of how they sometimes respond when things aren't going so well—when they aren't dancing on the ceiling.

When do we need to be interrupted by the Spirit?

As I write these words, I am sitting in my RV in a park on the northeast side of Jackson, MI.

I couldn't find a good place to write without interruptions (not interruptions of the Spirit, but the tedious ones you don't want when you are trying to accomplish something). So I went to the mobile office.

It is gorgeous outside. Chilly but clear. The tress have changed color. They are dropping leaves.

Across the park is a pond with geese. A little boy is feeding them bread and getting chased.

I'm laughing because I just got back from a walk where I was yelled at by the same geese.

As I was walking around the park, I got so caught up in it. It is easy to praise God when leaves are on fire and little boys are acting little-boyish.

It is easy to praise God in the middle of a park.

I found myself singing as I walked. I was actually singing out of Psalm 95, the part I learned as a kid, because it is fresh on my mind and I just wrote about it.

Then . . .

I started thinking about deadlines and getting this book done and interviewing job candidates and what time dinner is going to be and how I have to get the RV back to storage.

And I heard His voice.

It coaxed me to remember to pause, to take it in, to breathe deeply, to gain perspective.

It's not that the "stuff of life" doesn't matter—we need to work, we need to do our chores. And it's not that corporate worship helps us escape from those things. Rather, God wants our attention in the midst of all the mundane.

I have had a few conversations where people have said things to me like, "It must be wonderful to have a job where you get paid to worship and study about God and do spiritual things all the time."

Are you kidding me? Who wouldn't want that "job"? But it isn't reality. Not even for me.

Worship is a discipline. It's a choice. It's a perspective.

No matter if we work at a church, sell real estate, cut meat, drive a truck, work at the hospital, do home demonstrations for a direct sales company, or are currently working to find employment.

We worship as we work. We need perspective as we work. It's not about escape.

For this to happen, we need the spirit to interrupt us, not only while we are at work, but all the time.

Even in the middle of corporate worship.

We easily get caught up in the wonderful Wonka world of worship when everything is groovy and . . .

The Spirit interrupts us.

He wants us to remember.

What makes this interruption in Psalm 95 so interesting to me is that it sinterrupts *the corporate worship*. Imagine everyone singing a song out loud at church, and the music comes down, and the lights get dim, and the Spirit speaks. He gives a little insight, a little reminder, and points to something bigger and outside ourselves. He gives us context and perspective.

He doesn't want our empty words. He doesn't want shiny, happy, Jesus people. He wants spirit and truth worshippers.

It's like the Spirit is saying,

> "Hey, guys. I hear the singing. It is awesome. Keep it up. I love that you are all here together and of one mind. Now remember, this is the perspective I want for you all the time, even when you are in the suck. Remember that time when things didn't go so well and you were singing a different song? Let's not do that again. Hear my voice. Always. In it all. Through it all."

This King above all kings is our Maker. He carries us through, even when we test Him and make Him angry at times.

He wants our worship, our song, and our thanksgiving.

And

He wants us to listen.

    To His voice.

      To His reminders.

The King doesn't just want our words and tears in the chapel. He wants our contentment.

John Voelz

King Me

Section Three:

ELVIS AND THE COLONEL

Chapter Seven:

ROCK-A-HULA BABY

Sing to the Lord a new song;
sing to the Lord, all the earth.
Sing to the Lord, praise His name;
proclaim His salvation day after day.
Declare His glory among the nations,
His marvelous deeds among all peoples.

For great is the Lord and most worthy of praise;
He is to be feared above all gods.
For all the gods of the nations are idols,
But the Lord made the heavens.
Splendor and majesty are before Him;
Strength and glory are in His sanctuary.

Ascribe to the Lord, O families of nations,
ascribe to the Lord glory and strength.
Ascribe to the Lord the glory due His name;
bring an offering and come into His courts.
Worship the Lord in the splendor of His holiness;
tremble before Him, all the earth.

Say among the nations, "The Lord Reigns."
The world is firmly established, it cannot be moved;
He will judge the peoples with equity.
Let the heavens rejoice, let the earth be glad;
let the sea resound, and all that is in it;
let the fields be jubilant, and everything in them.
Then all the trees of the forest will sing for joy;
they will sing before the Lord, for He comes,
He comes to judge the earth.

He will judge the world in righteousness
and the peoples in His truth.

Psalm 96

According to some scholars, Psalm 96 may be the first in a section of the Kingly Psalms (96-99) that were written by the same author. By a cursory reading, it's easy to see why they came to this conclusion. The four psalms sound a lot alike, with similar phrases, wording, and flow.

At the same time, they are distinct from one another, and it may be unfair to look at them all at one time. Common sense says they are different songs, and though they may have ended up on the same album, we need to look at them as having their own message while at the same time sharing a theme. Like a rock and roll "concept album."

Sgt. Pepper's Lonely Heart's Club Band is my favorite Beatles album. It's unique in the Beatles' catalogue because it is a themed album or "concept album." The songs are supposed to go together: loosely, yes, but together nonetheless.

Often, you'll hear the first two songs on the album played together on the radio. "With a Little Help from my Friends" flows very nicely out of the title track.

Psalms 96-99 flow in much the same way, but they are also distinct from one another in the way that "Lucy in the Sky with Diamonds" is distinct from "Being for the Benefit of Mr. Kite."

If that last paragraph made no sense to you, I forgive you. For your penance, go listen to the *Sgt. Pepper's* album ten times through. Call me when you are done.

Just as Psalm 95 was quoted in Hebrews 3, one of the things that makes Psalm 96 stand out is its use in other parts of scripture; namely, 1 Chronicles 16, where verses 23-33 quote the psalm along with a potpourri of other psalms.

The song in 1 Chronicles quotes Psalms in the way an artist might sing a tribute montage at an awards show to honor someone's life—a little bit of this song, a little bit of that song form the catalogue.

Tribute songs pick songs for the montage that best suit the occasion. So at an awards show, Lady GaGa might do a montage to celebrate Elton John and sing parts of songs like Billy Joel's "Piano Man" or Roberta Flack's "Killing Me Softly" to draw attention to Elton's greatness and personality.

Or better yet, you might see something like what happened at Michael Jackson's funeral memorial celebration, where many different artists got together to sing Michael Jackson songs in their own style while trying to honor the man and the occasion.

So let's start by asking, "What is the occasion of 1 Chronicles 16, and why does it quote this psalm?" The answer to this will give us some insight as to the tone and appropriate setting for the psalm.

1 Chronicles 15-16 tells the story of the people of Israel bringing the Ark of the Covenant into Jerusalem. You may remember the ark from *Indiana Jones* if nowhere else. The ark was a rectangular box covered in gold that housed the two tablets of the law that were given to Moses (1 Kings 8:9), Aaron's rod (Numbers 17:1-10) and a jar holding manna (Exodus 16:32-34).

The ark has an exciting place in the history of Israel. It went through the desert with them as they traveled about, was stolen and fought over, and eventually returned to Jerusalem where David built a tent for it.

Finally David's son Solomon placed it in the holiest chamber of the temple he built.

The ark was a symbol of the presence of Yahweh on earth. Wherever the ark was, God was there. For this reason the Ark was brought into Jerusalem in 1 Chronicles 15-16.

The ark was a visible reminder to the people of their calling to be obedient to God and remember where they came from. The Ten Commandments on the tablets contained the law. Aaron's rod and the manna reminded them of times of complaining and grumbling and the Lord's provision and grace towards them.

The ark was covered with a lid often referred to as the "mercy seat" where two angels—cherubim—faced one another and guarded the presence of God.

The ark was a big deal. And this is why David brought it to Jerusalem to be placed in a tent where a celebration took place.

The importance of this event in history is felt today. It was significant in establishing Jerusalem not as a place of political power, but as a place of religious significance. In 1 Chronicles 16:4 we read,

> [David] appointed some of the Levites to minister before the ark of the Lord, to make petition, to give thanks, and to praise the Lord, the God of Israel . . .

King David established Jerusalem as a place of worship, and it continues to have that distinction today.

In ancient Israel, the king was God's representative on earth. A go-between. He spoke to the people as God's representative. But he was still a man.

The kings of Egypt were viewed as gods, but Israel's kings were seen as subjects and servants of Yahweh.

In 1 Chronicles 16, the king—a man—brings the ark into Jerusalem and sings songs to the King—Yahweh. As part of his montage of praise, he chooses a cutting from Psalm 96—a song about the King of the earth.

This psalm reflects the beauty and majesty of a King who has done great things, reminds all people of Israel to sing praises to Him and give Him worth, and reminds them of the duty they have to tell His story to the nations.

Yahweh loves families of nations, the whole earth, the world.

I think it's important to throw in a little side-note here about racism—of the past and today. We hear a lot of stories about how ancient Israel was ingrown and didn't care about surrounding nations. This is true to some extent, but it isn't the whole story. Israel had a call to tell the nations about Yahweh, and they celebrated that charge in song. We have no reason to believe that the people of Israel as a whole were only concerned for themselves. While there certainly was room for that sentiment in certain groups, we can safely assume they knew from the beginning that God had tasked them with being a light to all the world.

If we are honest, we probably have some anger towards certain people groups. Sometimes, our anger goes so deep that we lump many different people groups into one category of hatred. Perhaps we call to mind events like 9-11 and draw conclusions about all Muslims. Perhaps we find ourselves afraid on a train when sitting next to a group of people who look like the pictures we saw flashed on CNN the day a subway bomb went off.

The nation of Israel certainly had its share of racial intolerance, fear, anger, and prejudice. But we should take special note of the call we hear in the Psalms over and over again to love all nations and serve the King who loves all nations.

One of the things I love about reading the Psalms is the honesty of the songwriters' sentiment towards people groups that were doing them wrong. They had no problem in the First Testament praying "imprecatory prayers" where they asked God to bust people's faces.

But as we learned earlier, God was not in the business of simply beating up other nations who took Israel's lunch money. God has always had a plan to reveal himself to the world. Every one. Every people group.

Many praise songs today make use of the phrases "make God famous" and "tell of His fame" among the nations. It is a popular motif in modern worship music to recognize a particular country or people are not the only people Jesus died for. This is a return to the sentiment of early Psalms.

We see this plan come to fruition in the book of Revelation where a great multitude "from every nation, tribe, people, and language" stands before the throne of God and cries out in a loud voice,

> "Salvation belongs to our God,
> Who sits upon the throne,
> And to the Lamb."

Revelation 7:10

As a musician, I ask questions about the Psalms like 96 that I am pretty sure no one else asks:

What did early inventions and failed attempts at amplifiers look like for the musicians of the Psalms?

Was this one fast or slow?

Did they pull this off in 4/4 or 6/8? If it was 3/4, please don't tell me it was a waltz.

Would this be a guy or a girl solo part?

Would a sitar solo work nice here?

Is this verse/chorus/verse/chorus? Did it have repeats?

What guest musician would I hire for this song?
Who would produce this well? Danny Elfman? Brian Eno? Michael Gungor?

Was this a major or a minor key?

You get the picture.

Without getting into musical theory here which, quite frankly, would bore even me, the question of "major" or "minor" key might not be a bad one to ask.

If you aren't a trained musician, it might be easier to distinguish major and minor keys simply by their feel or by the way they make you feel.

Generally, songs in major keys are happy songs, the kinds of songs you usually sing out loud with your fist pumping in the air while smiling.

You may pump your fist at a rock anthem in a minor key as well, but you are probably also frowning or making a mean face.

Not that major key songs are bad by any means, but bubblegum pop songs usually lend themselves to the major keys (painting with large brush strokes here).

On the other hand, songs that are designed to make college girls cry like John Mayer's entire catalogue are usually minor key songs.

If you go to Westwinds Church, you probably have heard the song "Champion" (written by yours truly) many times over the years. It is a major key song (except for the cool minor bridge, which is an important point I am getting to soon).
You have no doubt also heard the song "Your Hand" (also written by me). This is a minor key song.

"Champion" is very lively. "Your Hand" is very mellow.

The words of "Champion" lend themselves to the major key because of the tone of the words. It just makes sense.

> I respond to all You are with all I am, You've taken hold
> O, Champion of my soul, my King, my God, my breath, my goal!

The words of "Your Hand" feel minor. They just do.

> Through tears, through pain, through loss, through the rain
> Your hand holds fast to me

All of this is to say, look at Psalm 96. It is good to wonder if it is major, minor, or both. Why? That question makes us wonder about the tone and helps us frame the song.

Other things that affect the feel of music are tempo and instrumentation. Fast songs are usually more spirited and happy. Slow songs are usually written to evoke either sad or serious moods. Or, once again, to get girls like John Mayer.

Violins sound like crying. They usually end up in sad or intense music. A tambourine is a happier percussive instrument. Penny Whistles are jolly and make you want to buy Irish Spring soap.

Key, tempo, and instrumentation set the tone of a song.

If you have an NIV study Bible, you may have noticed that verses 1-3 are grouped together, as well as 4-6; 7-9; and 10-13. This is because the editors of the NIV asked these very questions. They made these sections into stanzas or paragraphs as a little hint that something is going on. These groupings are *tone* distinctions. The stanzas are shown for you at the beginning of this chapter.

> The first stanza is about singing the praise of the King universally. Tell the world! God is marvelous!

> The second stanza is all about His splendor and majesty and strength and glory. His rule.

> The third mirrors the first—everyone, listen up!

> The fourth mirrors the second. He will not be shaken. He is the

King. He is the Judge.

If I were writing a musical score for this song, I might pick a major key for the first and third stanzas and a minor trail for the second and fourth.

The first and third stanzas are calls to action for us as worshipers. We have a job to do. Yes, they still talk about the nature of the King and point to the King, but these sections give us the "So what does that mean for us?" parts of the song.

We sing.

    We shout.

        We worship.
           We bring offerings.

                We tell.

                    We tremble before him.

                        We proclaim.

                          We declare.

Worship is not passive for the believer. It is a call to action. It is a major key celebration of putting feet to our faith. It is not hidden behind stained glass windows or, as the case may be at Westwinds, in a black box theatre with crazy, changing, funky and creative aesthetics.

At Westwinds, we often talk about worship in terms of "responding to all that God is with all that we are." I even included that instruction in the song "Champion" listed above.

God has pursued mankind through the ages. When God said, "I Am," to Moses, He was telling us He would be everything He is to His people. God initiates a relationship with us. God makes Himself known to us, expresses His character and intentions to us.

This demands a response.

Because He is worthy of it.

We are in a stage of life with our pre-teen daughter right now where we are looking for a certain kind of response that just isn't happening all the time. She is getting better, but . . .
The response we are looking for is that self-motivation that comes without being told to do something. Why? Because that's what we do—we help out. We do our chores. We pitch in. We don't whine.

This is a part of life we all go through. We went through it with our other children, so I don't feel bad telling stories about her right now. It isn't her issue; it's everyone's issue.

The response we are looking for is one that should come automatically for someone who realizes what she has and who gave it to her. The response we are looking for is one of respect for parents who love their children and pour themselves out for them. The response we are looking for is one of self-realization.

We don't want a robot in the house. We want a team player who is motivated out of love for the family and a mutual respect of others' things and roles and such.

I'm reminded of a scene from the movie *The Break-Up* with Jennifer Aniston and Vince Vaughn. In the kitchen of the apartment Aniston and Vaughn share, they are arguing over the dishes. The poignant and painful line Aniston says to Vaughn is,

> "I don't want you to do the dishes. I want you to want to do the dishes."

This line fueled women everywhere, giving them a catchphrase to use over and over again. It has ruined countless relationships since the release of the movie and will live forever in eternity.

But it's a good picture of what the psalmist is saying and what God wants from us with our worship. He isn't giving us tasks like little puppies to perform: "Roll over!" "Bark!" "Sit, Ubu, sit. Good dog."

He wants us to worship because we want to worship.

And this is where my movie analogy breaks down. Washing dishes is a chore, something to get out of the way so you can messy them up again. Worship is not a chore. It is a way of living, seeing, hearing, responding.

God reveals who He is throughout all scripture. He reveals who we are to ourselves. In the story of the woman at the well we mentioned a few chapters earlier (John 4), she responded by running and telling all her friends, "Come see a man who told me everything I ever did. Could this be the Christ?" We should do the same. "Come and see!"

John 4 says, "Many of the Samaritans from that town believed in him because of the woman's testimony." When the people of that area hung out with Jesus, they said to the woman, "We no longer believe just because of what you said; now we have heard for ourselves, and we know that this man really is the Savior of the world." And round and round it goes.

There is an element of worship that is evangelistic in nature.

Unfortunately, the word "evangelism" has garnered a bad reputation in recent years. I believe this is mostly because of idiots who beat people over the head with their bibles, questions, and scare tactics to the extent that the evangelized want to go Miyagi-son on the evangelists' behinds.

When I say worship is evangelistic I am not talking about this kind of a militant persuasive assault and I am not talking about evangelism as a flip-chart presentation.

"Do you love Him? Mark yes or no."

Yuck.

I'm not talking about evangelism in terms of some one act passion play where we try to seal the deal by the end.

No.

I am certainly not talking about anything that has to do with a bull horn or a sandwich board that screams, "The end is near," or "Turn or burn."

I wish those people would stop speaking for me. Yahweh is not about guilt motivation, hatred, or scare tactics.
I'm speaking of the kind of "evangelism" that makes people ask, "Why do you love me so much?"

The words "evangelism" and "gospel" come from the same root word that means "good headlines." What is happening in Psalm 96 is just that. Good headlines followed up by a response. The nations watch. They hear. They observe. They follow. Because everyone wants to hear good news.

Good news does not require a beating.

Psalm 96 is a celebration. The King is here. He has done good things. We are here to worship Him.

Watch us!

Join us!

Everyone!

Chapter Eight:

IN THE GHETTO

The Lord reigns, let the earth be glad;
let the distant shores rejoice.
Clouds and thick darkness surround Him;
righteousness and justice are the foundation of His throne.
Fire goes before Him
and consumes His foes on every side.
His lightning lights up the world;
the earth sees and trembles.
The mountains melt like wax before the Lord,
before the Lord of all the earth.
The heavens proclaim His righteousness,
and all the peoples see His glory.
All who worship images are put to shame,
those who boast in idols—
worship Him all you gods!
Zion hears and rejoices
and the villages of Judah are glad
because of Your judgments, O Lord.
For You, O Lord, are the Most High over all the earth;
You are exalted far above all gods.
Let those who love the Lord hate evil,
for He guards the lives of His faithful ones
and delivers them from the hand of the wicked.
Light is shed upon the righteous
and joy on the upright in heart.
Rejoice in the Lord, you who are righteous,
and praise His holy name.

Psalm 97

I love the video of Elvis singing "In the Ghetto" to a crowded auditorium full of nicely dressed people eating good food and having cocktails while Elvis is displayed in all his collar-popped, sideburned, hairy-chested glory.

I have no problem with enjoying the good things of life. I have no problem with celebration and enjoying fine wine or with a bit of shimmer and gold. I just find the contrast between the song and the setting interesting.

I'm not putting Elvis down—for all I know, he could have been singing for a charity auction. Still . . . the contrast.

The bigger contrast however, is between Elvis and the people. No matter how nicely dressed they are, they don't match up to the grandeur of Elvis in all his decadence.

I see the same kind of contrasts when I read Psalm 97. It is full of things that are juxtaposed to one another—righteousness and evil, light and dark, power and weakness.

The psalm contains a bunch of rather dark and scary poetic descriptions of the glory of Yahweh, combined with a proclamation of worship, combined with warnings to people who worship idols, culminating in light being shed on the righteous.

It is frightening and jubilant at the same time.

We are told to be "glad" because of the reign of The King and to "rejoice," followed by images and word pictures of something akin to The Great and Powerful Oz (when he was scary with a big green head).

We are supposed to feel these contrasts.

All of the contrasting images and language serve to support and strengthen one very large idea:

There is a King. We are not Him.

It is difficult to describe The King. Words do not do Him justice. Poetry is an attempt to fill in the gaps.

But there are gaps.

First, the poet of Psalm 97 uses the most powerful image he can think of to describe the reign and coming judgment of The King: the imagery of a fierce thunderstorm.

The clouds that fill up the sky and block out the sun surround Him like a veil and temporarily block the world from His judgment. His judgment is likened to a storm raging with lightning that strikes down and consumes with fire. The fire is so hot that it melts mountains like wax.

All of this happens as the world—the people who are subservient to The King—watches and worships.

Much of this psalm echoes back to our earlier conversation about being able to rejoice in The King's justice and judgment over evil. Remember, we are not rejoicing in someone else's pain and suffering, we are rejoicing that God ultimately will eradicate the world of evil.

Let those who love the Lord hate evil.

There is great comfort in this because . . .

. . . He guards the lives of His faithful ones and delivers them from the hand of the wicked.

Because of this elimination of evil and the ultimate protection of The King's people, His people rejoice.

"Light is shed upon the righteous and joy on the upright in heart. Rejoice in the Lord, you who are righteous, and praise His holy name."

The contrast between wickedness and righteousness is like opening the blinds in a dark room for the sunlight to make its deluge. The darkness is dark but it holds no power over the light. The evil is evil but it will not withstand the judgment.

No person, no ideology, no rebellion can stand up to the King.

Another contrast in this psalm describes what is happening on land and what is happening in heaven—the earth and the clouds, the mountains and the sky, Zion and Judah (the people down here) and the Most High over all (the God up there).

In the Psalms, "Zion" is a name used to describe the dwelling place of The King. (Psalm 2, 48, 110). It is referred to as the Holy Mountain (2, 3, 15, 43, 99). It is a sanctuary and refuge (15, 20, 78). It is where the saints worship (9, 48, 65, 99, 102, 137, 150). The King dwells there (3, 9, 50, 65, 74, 76, 128, 133). It is a city or a land (2, 48, 51, 69, 78, 87, 97, 102). Help comes from Zion (9, 14, 20). It is a symbol of majesty for all to see (2, 48, 50). It is an everlasting land and kingdom (125, 48, 132). All followers of Yahweh are citizens of Zion.

When scripture mentions Zion, it refers to many things, depending on the context. True, Zion has a geographic location, but its theological significance is much broader.

It also refers to a people,

The King's heavenly realm,

the presence of The King with his people,

strength, refuge, and a place of citizenship—

a land where we belong.

I always love hearing different countries' national anthems being played at Olympic Games ceremonies. I love to see the pride on athletes' faces when the song of their land is played. I love to root for Team U.S.A. but, in the end, the Olympic Games are not only about national pride. They are about pride in the human race—living and playing in harmony.

In much the same way that the Olympic Games celebrate country as well as all of humanity, Psalm 97 celebrates Zion *and* all the peoples of the world who find their identity in Yahweh—the "Most High over all the earth." The national anthem of Zion is one for all the peoples.

Zion is eternal and accessible no matter where you are or who you are. Yahweh is not restricted to one land. Worship and connection with this land is a state of the heart. Citizenship in Zion is related to character and heart. Spirit and truth.

The people of Zion rejoice in God's judgment not because of who is left out or who doesn't get to participate. It isn't a vindictive rejoicing. The people can rejoice because they belong. And everyone has a chance to belong, to avoid the inevitable judgment. Everyone is offered escape.

The contrast in Psalm 97 is not between different kinds of people, it is between *all people of the earth* and Yahweh.

Citizens of Zion and those who are not yet citizens are *all* dependent on the One who is "Most High over all the earth."

The all-inclusive words of Psalm 97 serve as a reminder to everyone that God is not a respecter of one certain group of people. Some of the most horrific wars and injustices have risen out of ideologies that elevate one group of people as sovereign over another.

The people of First Testament Israel needed a reminder that it wasn't all about them and Yahweh's plan is to draw *all* nations and people to Himself.

We need the same reminder.

I have heard some people go to great lengths to point out the militant nationalism and exclusive pride that existed in First Testament Israel but it is unfair to make that sentiment indicative of *all* the people of First Testament Israel. It is no more fair than saying all U.S. Americans believe they are more special than the rest of the world.

We all have potential for misplaced identity. Psalm 97 reminds us of who and what we are. And who we are not.

I'm always saddened when people confuse nationalism and religion. Over the years Christians have had a great deal of pride in America being a Christian land. We claim a religious past, celebrate the Christian values of our forefathers, put "In God we trust" on our money, and take great pride in our Puritan settler's heritage.

We call ourselves a Christian nation.

Truth be told, while some of our founding fathers were deeply religious and some would argue the most capable generation of statesmen ever to appear in America, they were not specifically Christian.

According to the authors of *The Search for Christian America*, some of our founding fathers were orthodox Christians—like John Jay and Patrick Henry; virtually all of them had a profound belief in "the supreme judge of the world" and the "protection of divine providence"; but many were Deists—men who believed in a Supreme Deity who made a clock and set it on a shelf and didn't intervene with human affairs.

They were self-made men. They believed God created mankind with potential and great skill to rule. To make his own way. To create an ideal and more perfect land.

How are we doing?

There is no such thing as a Christian nation. Well-intentioned statesmen do not make a Christian nation. The Ten Commandments on the wall of classrooms do not make a Christian nation.

A Christian president does not equal a Christian nation. A Christian president says something about his identity but not yours.

Not mine.

Not ours.

So where do all the people of the world go to find their identity?

The people of Zion from Jerusalem "to the distant shores" find their identity in King Yahweh. They rejoice in His great and powerful judgment, knowing things will one day be set right and that He provides a haven for those who see Him as righteous and submit to His authority.

John Voelz

Chapter Nine:

HEARTBREAK HOTEL

A Psalm.

Sing to the Lord a new song,
for He has done marvelous things;
His right hand and His holy arm
have worked salvation for Him.
The Lord has made His salvation known
and revealed His righteousness to the nations.
He has remembered His love
and His faithfulness to the house of Israel;
all the ends of the earth have seen the salvation of our God.

Shout for joy to the Lord, all the earth,
burst into jubilant song with music;
make music to the Lord with the harp,
with the harp and the sound of singing,
with trumpets and the blast of the ram's horn,
shout for joy before the Lord, the King.

Let the sea resound and everything in it.
Let the rivers clap their hands,
let the mountains sing together for joy;
let them sing before the Lord,
for He comes to judge the earth.
He will judge the world in righteousness
And the peoples with equity.

Psalm 98

For the last few chapters, we've done a combination of biblical exegesis, exploring Hebrew poetry, and revisiting history.

Now I would like to talk frankly for a few pages just have a discussion about something I think needs to be said. Heart to heart.

For the second time (there are three in total) in our look at these Kingly Psalms, we see that Psalm 98 is designated as "A Psalm." Remember this means it is supposed to be played with instruments and maybe a choir. It's big. And it is most often associated with "praise" songs in scripture.

This designation makes sense, since the psalm mentions the harp, the trumpets, and the ram's horn.

I am going to be a little cynical here. I'm telling you before I even get started so you won't call me on it. I'm admitting it to you because I'm not sure it will come out right. I don't know how to edit myself. And I'm not sure I should anyway. Here goes . . .

I'm not the only one who sees there is a lot of music going on here, right? Singing, shouting, loudness. It all seems pretty straightforward. Psalm 98 is full of singing, rejoicing, and a playful freedom in praising Yahweh.

This "obvious" recognition and some people's inability to see it has been the cause of weirdness for me in my life as a musician.

I grew up in a church in Northern California. It wasn't the first church I was part of, nor the second, but it was the church I did most of my growing up in. My wife grew up there as well. I started going there because she was there. I led music for the youth group. A lot of wonderful people there helped shape me and spoke into my life.

But when it came to music, they were so screwy (in my twenty-four year-old mind).

We had a blast in the youth group. We had lots of instruments. We had a sound system. Amps. Drums. It was great. And though we didn't know what we were doing, it seemed pretty Biblical, with shouting singing, and making noises by hitting stuff.

One day, we were asked to share some music in what we liked to call "big church." By this time, I was an adult—young, but an adult. I was in charge of music for the high school group. I agreed to share music with the big church.

I was twenty-four years old newly married and loved spending time with the high school kids. I was barely out of high school myself and full of energy.

Oblivious.

Naïve.

Dumb.

The Sunday we were asked to share our musical "gifts" with the congregation was a choir Sunday. On choir Sundays, which came around every few weeks, the choir stood up front in their robes and led us through a few hymns.

I got there early to set up the stage (choirs just walk on stage, but rock and roll takes a whole crew of roadies and about two hours to get ready).

The stage was set with two guitars, a bass, a keyboard, and drums. It looked awesome. The stage was barely big enough to hold all the weapons that would liberate people on the front lines of rock and roll.

The choir had been rehearsing down the hall in the choir room (they had their own space), and they started heading down the hall. I stood there high-fiving some people I knew who were in the choir like they were coming out of the locker room tunnel of an NBA game. We were in this together!

So I thought.

I was not prepared for what happened next. Being young at this, I had no context. Even though I had been playing music for youth since I was fifteen or so, I had never brought this setup into big church.

I had been turned down as a musician in my parents' church, but that made more sense to me. That context was like church prison. My parents' church (that has now fallen apart, by the way) didn't like anything. Everything and everybody was suspect. In hindsight, at twenty-four, I could look back and laugh. That old church was dysfunction junction, but things HAD to be different here . . . right?

Nope.

In this corner, weighing in at 150 pounds, guitar slung over his shoulder, is "The Friend of Fellowship Funk," "The Ayatollah of Jesus Rock n Rollah," "The Minister of Rock and Roll" . . . Mr. John Voelz.

And in this corner, weighing in at a heavy amount of disdain and angst, robed and ready for battle, "The Mothers of Molten Madness,"

"The Ladies of the 1680's," "The Keepers of the Cantata" . . . the choir ladies!

I'm having fun here to work through my pain.

One lady came around the corner and pointed to the stage as she put her arm around another lady.

They both started crying.

Apparently no one had told them in advance that this was happening. They began to get very upset. They pointed at me and shook their heads.

Another lady came around the corner and, I kid you not . . . threw up. Vomited. Puked. Right there in the hallway.

Now I had heard that some may not have been particularly fond of the loud rock and roll that was coming from down the hall. I was aware that some were not keen on us covering old rock and roll tunes as kids walked in or actually singing secular music in the church. But I was not prepared for the Adventures of Weepy Lady and Barf Girl.

"There's drums in there!" said Barf Girl. "Why? Why?" I kid you not. She said, "Why?" twice, like they do in the movies.

I was invited to join the elders for a meeting. They didn't have the greatest things to say. They weren't mean, but they made it known what side they were on. I remember one of them saying, "It's just not worth fighting about. We've tried to change some things, but I guess this is who we are."

Heartbreak Hotel.

I wondered if I would ever be in a church where I could experience the playful freedom in worship like I read about in Psalm 98.

For the next twenty years, I would spend much of my energy fighting what are commonly referred to as "the worship wars." In these wars (and make no mistake, they are battles), debates rage and arrows are hurled (usually in the direction of younger musicians and non-traditional music) over what is too loud, too fast, too complicated, too wordy, not wordy enough, too repetitive, too similar to an old song about sex, too gratuitous, too self-centered, lacking appropriate direct references to scripture, lacking the use of the name Jesus, and so on.

I like to think I served well in the years I was enlisted in the battle of the worship wars. I like to think I had good motivation for change and progress. I hope that most of the time I was kind and had a teachable attitude as much as I had an axe to grind.

But I know I failed to keep my cool sometimes. And, honestly, while the worship wars brought about great perspective and new methodologies for the church at large, many of us spent too many years and too much energy on the wrong battlefield. If we would have spent half as much energy taking our songs of redemption to the rest of the world rather than fighting about what we could play in church, I can't imagine the kind of revival we would have seen.

Throughout the Kingly Psalms, the songwriters tell us to sing new songs about the marvelous King and make His name known throughout the earth. Some need to hear that message in a country song. Some will be attracted to that message through a singer-songwriter in a bar with a guitar. Or through Bluegrass. Or Punk.

Psalm 98 mentions some funky instrumentation that I don't believe is a recipe for this particular song or any specific song for that matter. The harp, the singing, the trumpet, the ram's horn . . . this is all poetic speech like we talked about in chapter two.

Pairing groups of words like this are a poetic way to convey totality in the same way we might tell someone to bring their hats, coats, mittens, long-johns and Snuggies to the outdoor football game . It's a much more fun and poetic way of saying, "Whatever you play, bring it here! Let's make music for the King." It all goes. God has blessed it all and welcomes it all.

The worship wars have died out to a great degree. Some churches continue to carry a lot of bitterness and anger over styles of music, but for the most part, the carnage has all been carried off the battlefield. After a while, people started realizing it wasn't a battle worth fighting.

Don't get me wrong, no one conceded. No one gave up. Everyone just started new churches. And this is one of the greatest things that ever came out of those battles. More people got reached in the process. God used our bickering for good.

The worship wars helped us all learn a little something along the way.

I'm older now. I have been a musician in the church for twenty-seven years. I have new perspective. I have simmered down. I see things more clearly. Here are a few things I learned through the process:

1. *Style and preferences in music don't matter*. Not in the big picture. They matter to an individual and that is okay. You are free to have your own musical identity. But yours isn't right. And neither is mine.

Choirs are cool for some and horribly wrong for others. Loud rock and roll is the bees knees for some and terrible for others. It's okay.

2.   *The King gives freedom.* Corporate worship music and all the other participatory things in corporate worship are not prescriptive in scripture. If they were, we should all be doing songs in church with harps, trumpets, cymbals, and ram's horns.

3.   *Jesus is the common denominator.* When you go into a church, you should ask, "What do I have in common with these folks?" You should stay away from, "How am I different?" You may not like everything that happens at your church but it's not all about you. Someone else likes it, probably a lot of people, or they wouldn't be there.

4.   *Prepare for worship.* I am convinced (and so is scripture) that the worship experience is participatory and not a spectator sport. Pray before coming together with others to worship. Immerse yourself in scripture. Ask God for perspective. Then, dig in.

You will get out what you put in. If you fight to get the kids into the car, yell at your wife or husband on the way, drive one hundred miles an hour to church and expect to get swept away in the wonderful world of worship, you may be disappointed.

5.   *Don't complain.* It gets you nowhere. No matter where you go to church, the leaders are picking songs they think

are good. You are not going to change that. If you are at a church where you don't particularly like the style of some worship element, you have two choices: be quiet and supportive or leave. But leavers beware: no church will be your perfect mix of everything you like.

6. *Somebody else will always pick the songs.* Unless you are the person who picks them, and there are only a few of us, you are along for the ride. I can say this because I also discipline myself to be in other situations where I have to submit to someone else's song choices.

    This is one of the reasons I go to conferences or visit churches on vacation. Great discipline and perspective comes with submission to someone else's playlist. The psalmists never say, "Join in if you like the song." They simply say, "Sing!"

7. *Expanding your musical horizons is a great discipline.* You would be hard-pressed to guess what kind of music I like by looking at my CD collection.

    At the time I am writing this, there are nearly 13,000 songs in my iTunes playlist. I could hit "play" and listen to music without stopping for over two years and never hear the same song twice.

    In all honesty, some of the songs I lead at church I don't like a whole lot. But I listen to people around me, and when a song hits a nerve and a lot of people like it, I give it a shot.

Sometimes songs get old for me, and my team tells me, "Please keep this one!"

Listening to a great variety of music has enabled me to learn to respect and in some cases find a love for new styles I wouldn't naturally gravitate towards. I dare you to do the same.

My friend Jeremy is a pastor in a church denomination called The Church of Christ. Actually, they are not technically a denomination but a loose affiliation of churches that hold common beliefs.

The Churches of Christ have some interesting ideas I won't get into here, but a small amount of searching the web should clue you in. For example, though these independent churches differ in practices, there is usually a common thread with a disregard for the creeds, a belief that the church should not support para-church organizations and a model based on what they believe the Second Testament Church looked like.

One particular branch of The Churches of Christ forbids any musical instruments in worship because the Second Testament does not specifically refer to instruments in worship. Jeremy is the pastor of a church in this branch.

Though I think they make an argument out of silence, I don't find it necessary to waste any time arguing with this group of people who love Jesus. (The Second Testament doesn't say they used light bulbs to illuminate their churches, but that doesn't mean I want to sit in the dark.) I think they are wrong, but we can still have coffee together.

Jeremy loves music. He's a U2 fan like me. We have lunch every once in awhile and chat about ministry. And music.

Jeremy feels called to pastor these people at this time. In some ways, he is totally out of his element. But what I love and admire about Jeremy is his ability to put aside his differences for a few hours a week to be able to do life with a group of people who have different ideas about worship style.

They sing at church. But there is no Larry Mullen Jr. on the drums or The Edge on Guitar or Adam Clayton on bass. There is just the sound of singing. And . . . that's okay. I think they are missing out on some great things, but in the grand scope of things and shadowing God in the redemption of the world, to each his own.

I have visited *a cappella* churches before. I wouldn't want to stay there, but I have had wonderful experiences worshipping with other voices. I hope they could show up at my church and find some common ground as well.

I think there is a special spot in heaven for Jeremy. There is a giant theatre with quality sound where great music plays all day long. On the wall is a sign hand-painted by God that says, "Thanks for going with the flow and focusing on what matters."

One more thing in regard to Psalm 98:. If we take a close look at the first couple of verses, we notice something special. The call is for us to sing: not just any song, but a special kind of a song, because of a special aspect of The King's character.

We are told to sing a new song.

New.

Because of His salvation.

The word translated here as "salvation" is the word *ye su ah*. This same word is also translated in other parts of the First Testament as "savior," "deliverance," and "deliverer."

Check this out . . .

It is where the name "Joshua" or "Jeshua" comes from. The name "Joshua" means literally, "Yahweh is salvation" or "Yahweh delivers" as it combines both the abbreviated name of God, "Yahweh," and "ye su ah."

The name "Joshua" or "Jeshua" is a Hebrew name. Moses' successor was named Joshua. Moses gave him that name prior to his leading the Hebrew people into the promised land (his original name was Hoshea or Hosea). This seems a fitting new name for a person who leads God's people to victory (*ye su ah* is also translated "victory" in some places in scripture).

It is also a fitting name for another leader. Another victorious one. Another that proclaimed "Yahweh is salvation."

Jesus. The Christ.

The Greek name "Jesus" is the equivalent of the Hebrew "Joshua." To Jesus' playground friends, He would have been known as Joshua. It is the Greek translation of the name that gives us "Jesus."

Psalm 98 tells us to sing a new song because of salvation that God brings (and did bring, and will bring) to the nations.

In a playful way, it is not out of the realm of possibility that Psalm 98 points the people to sing and look forward to coming salvation. That salvation is finally seen in the person of Jesus, whose very name means exactly what is being sung about.

The word "new" as in "sing a new song" is also translated as "fresh" or "recently" and is closely related to the word translated "renew" or "restore."

The Hebrew people were instructed to bring everything they had to the place of corporate worship.

> Praise The King for His salvation—what He has done and what He will do.

> Sing with fresh perspective. Sing songs about your recent experience. Tell everyone.

> It's not about you. It's about The King.

Chapter Ten:

WALK A MILE IN MY SHOES

The Lord reigns,
let the nations tremble;
He sits enthroned between the cherubim,
let the earth shake.
Great is the Lord in Zion;
He is exalted over all the nations.
Let them praise Your great and awesome name—
He is holy.
The King is mighty, He loves justice—
You have established equity;
in Jacob You have done
what is just and right.
Exalt the Lord our God
and worship at His footstool—
He is holy.
Moses and Aaron were among His priests,
Samuel was among those who called on His name;
they called on the Lord
and He answered them.
He spoke to them from the pillar of cloud;
they kept His statutes and the decrees He gave them.
O Lord, our God,
You answered them;
You were to Israel a forgiving God,
though You punished their misdeeds.
Exalt the Lord our God
and worship at His holy mountain,
for the Lord our God is holy.

Psalm 99

Based on everything we have learned thus far, take some time and do a little exegesis yourself. You have the technology. You have the tools.

Do some observation of Psalm 99 and start asking questions about it. Who? What? When? Where? Why? How? Look for repetition. Look for poetic device. Grab a pen, maybe a couple of different translations of the Bible (NIV, NAS, NASB, KJV), get access to the internet, and do some exploration.

I will give you a few questions to guide you along your way.

1.   Why does the psalm mention cherubim? Why is God "enthroned between them"? What do you know about cherubim? Have we mentioned them before?

2.   What does the psalmist mean by "Zion" in this context?

3.   Who is Jacob and why might he be important here? What did
        he do? Did he do something wrong? Is there a story associated
        with him? A promise?

4.   Where or what is The King's footstool?

5.   Are there any repeated words or phrases here? Does anything
        sound familiar?

6.   Can you recognize any poetic structure here? Do you see any poetic devices? Where is there a chiasm (hint: maybe an A - B - A kind of a structure)?

7.   We've talked a bit about Moses and Aaron. Why is Samuel mentioned here? Who was he (hint: read about priests and prophets)? Was Moses really a priest, or is that a poetic device? What do they all have in common?

8.   Where is The King's holy mountain? When did God speak through a pillar of cloud? Will he ever do that again? Did it happen more than once?

Chapter Eleven:

I Can't Help Falling in Love With You

A psalm. For giving thanks.

Shout for joy to the Lord, all the earth.
Worship the Lord with gladness;
come before Him with joyful songs.
Know that the Lord is God.
It is He who made us and we are His;
we are His people, the sheep of His pasture.

Enter His gates with thanksgiving
and His courts with praise;
give thanks to Him and praise His name.
For the Lord is good and His love endures forever;
His faithfulness continues through all generations.

Psalm 100

Next to Psalm 93, which is also five verses, this is the shortest and the last psalm in our series of Kingly Psalms. And whether or not the Psalm was written specifically for the purpose of closing out a section of the Kingly Psalms, it has been traditionally regarded as the cap—as the other bookend.

It makes sense that this should be the finale. This psalm is a celebration of celebrations. If it were a rock show, the stage would be cleared, the people would be stomping their feet and pumping their fists, the lights would be down, and suddenly the band would return for an encore—Psalm 100! Chucka-shraaaaaaang . . . (that's the phonetic rendering of the sound a guitar makes when the guitarist hits one chunky power chord to start the encore).

I love encores. They are highly predictable in live shows today. Once upon a time, a band would leave the stage with no intention of returning and then the crowd would go wild, start tossing chairs, and scream, "We want more!" or various chants like "El-vis! El-vis! El-vis!" until the band walked on stage and did one final song.

As predictable as encores are today, I love the anticipation. I love the feel when the stadium goes dark and cell phones start waving back and forth. I love the sound of the people chanting. I love the feeling that something great is about to happen.

When I go to shows with my son, we like to guess which song the band will start with. In the same way, we guess which song or songs will be played for the encore. What you start with is important, but your ending is even more important. The ending is what everyone will remember.

The band will most definitely want to pick a favorite as the ending— something that is easily accessible something everyone can join in and sing with arms locked and eyes closed.

If you are in a one-hit-wonder band, you'd better end on that one song that made you famous. Or make sure you do a cover of someone else's song and make it sound really cool.

When the blog writers start the chatter about the show, be sure they will talk about the encore.

The phrase, "Elvis has left the building," has become a popular funny line in modern pop culture, but it came from an actual announcement made over the system at Elvis concerts so people would go home instead of lingering in the concert halls praying Elvis would do another encore.

Elvis was anything but a one-hit-wonder and often did encores of whatever song he wanted. Whatever he picked was the right one. He was the King of Rock and Roll.
He could fart in a microphone and girls would faint.

But Elvis gave his encores great thought. His encores changed throughout the years, but "I Can't Help Falling in Love with You" was a favorite. Elvis was a rock and roller, but he was more about girls. Just watch his movies. Elvis chose wisely. A band's encore, like Elvis's, should sum up what the artist is all about.

The writer of Psalm 100 chose wisely as well.

The superscription tells us this is a psalm for thanksgiving. It is very possible this was a psalm designed for a festival or specific celebration, but it fits anywhere it is sung.

This psalm does not specifically mention The King, but is thought to be a denouement, an encore, and a finale to The Kingly Psalms. This is the psalm that says, "This is what you are going home with."

So here we are. At the end.

And what matters?

Thank Him.

Shout for joy. Bring it on. Everything you have within you.

You were made by Him.

You have a place in the kingdom.

He watches over you.

You have a welcome invitation.

He isn't going anywhere.

Writing thank you notes is a big deal in our house. I am horrible at it. Our kids are horrible too. My wife is awesome. She always has to remind us.

I've gotten better over the years, but I have to discipline myself. I have to put a date on the calendar, sit with a stack of cards, and make a list of all the people I want to thank. I love to get thank you cards, so I assume everyone else does as well.

There is nothing quite like a handwritten note that is specific in its thanks.

Thank you for the time you spent with me.

The words of encouragement were thoughtful.

I love it when you said . . .

Have you sat down recently and made a list of the things you are thankful for? It's a great discipline and a real perspective changer if you are open to it.

The King is appreciative of your thanks.

I know a person (who will remain nameless) who always hints at the fact that they want to be thanked, and it drives me nuts. "Did you see the note I left?" "Did you get the gift?" "I just wanted to make sure everything was okay, because I recently sent you something and I hadn't heard from you."

The King isn't looking for that kind of thanks. He isn't begging for recognition. He isn't looking for flattery.

He is looking for unity among His people. He's looking for a throng of people to come together in purpose. He's looking for a celebration.

He's looking for a people to come together in such a way that when they give thanks and live together in unity, the world looks on, enraptured by The King, because they see what He has done through a people.

There is no time to bicker when we are giving thanks.

We all need each other for this. We need to remind each other. We need to hold each other accountable.

We are the king-dom.

One of the big unspoken themes of the Kingly Psalms is a coming together of The King's people. There is unity, purpose, and one-mindedness when the people of The King come together, when they share stories, remember, and make a loud noise.

These psalms are not songs you sing from the Bible you keep on the back of your toilet.

They are personal, however, when you allow them to wash over you and speak to you, when you allow the weightiness of what is being said edit your own experience.

In the same way we talked about the Holy Spirit co-writing Psalms, the Holy Spirit wants to be your co-writer of a life lived for The King. Your life is a song. A poem.
Really.

Ephesians 2:10 says,

> For we are God's workmanship, created in Christ Jesus to do good works, which God prepared in advance for us to do.

The word "workmanship" is a translation of the word *poiema*. It's the same word we get "poem" from. Your life is a poem.

What does it say?

What will it say?

What do you want it to say?

In some ways, your poem is already written. And in many ways, you are an open book. With an invitation from a King.

To listen.

To Him, yes, but also to the others in the kingdom.

To join in and hide no longer.

To celebrate.

    To surrender.

        To be a singer-shouter-storyteller.

      For the King.

One King remains.

Notes On Biblical Poetry:

Below are some things to look for in biblical poetry that you can refer back to as you study the Kingly Psalms, and any psalm for that matter (*all the questions and examples in this next section are from Ray Lubeck of Multnomah Bible College and Seminary, used with his permission, and are not to be reprinted*).

Things to Look for in Biblical Poetry

Question: What is poetry?
Poetry is a form of writing where normal language is changed to intensify its impact. Poetry is a "kind of language that says more and says it more intensely than does ordinary language" (taken from *Sound and Sense: An Introduction to Poetry* by Laurence Perrine).

Question: What are some ways this is done in English?
Often English poetry uses rhyme or rhythm (meter):
>Roses are red
>Violets are blue
>Sugar is sweet
>And so are you

Poetry also "bends" the normal rules of grammar, punctuation, and word order.

>Out of the fertile ground he caused to grow
>All trees of noblest kind for sight, smell, taste;
>And all amid them stood the Tree of Life,

High eminent, blooming ambrosial fruit
Of vegetable gold; and next to life,
Our death, the Tree of Knowledge, grew fast by—
Knowledge of good, bought dear by knowing ill.

John Milton, *Paradise Lost*

Question: How is it usually done in biblical poetry?
The key feature of biblical poetry is parallelism. Parallelism is the "rhyming" of thoughts and forms rather than sounds.

The grave	*cannot*	*praise you*
Death	*cannot*	*sing your praise.*

Isaiah 38:18

There are several kinds of biblical parallelism:

Synonymous: The thought of the 1st line is repeated in the second.

Yahweh is my light and my salvation	*whom*	*shall I fear?*
Yahweh is the stronghold of my life	*of whom*	*shall I be afraid?*

Psalm 27:1

I will sing	*to Yahweh*	*all my life*
I will sing praise	*to my God*	*as long as I live*

Psalm 104:33

Antithetic: The 2nd line states the opposite of the 1st line.

The prospect | of the righteous | is joy
But the hopes | of the wicked | come to nothing

Proverbs 10:28

Yahweh | tears down | the proud man's | house
But He | keeps | the widow's | boundaries intact

Proverbs 15:25

Inverted: The parts in the 2nd line are in reverse order from the 1st.

O Yahweh, | do not forsake me
Be not far from me, | O my God

Psalm 38:21

Synthetic: The 2nd line simply builds on the idea of the first.

You broaden the path beneath me
So that my ankles do not turn.

Psalm 18:36

Also, when looking at parallelism, notice the use of what is referred to as **ellipsis**.

Ellipses: Frequently the second line will omit an implied element from the first line:

May Yahweh	*cut off*	*all flattering lips*	
And ---	*---*	*every boasting tongue*	

Psalm 12:3

Here you naturally understand the implied subject (Yahweh) and verb (will cut off) from the first line and import it into the second line. This omission is called an ellipsis. Most often, when one or two elements are missing, they are compensated for by an added, different element in the second line.

To bind	*their kings*	*with fetters*	*---*
---	*their nobles*	*with shackles*	***of iron***

Psalm 149:8

For You	*O God*	*tested us*	*---*
You	*---*	*refined us*	***like silver***

Psalm 66:10

These added words serve to balance out the length of the two lines, and are sometimes referred to as a "ballast."

Sometimes the corresponding elements are simply lengthened to compensate for the missing element.

Yahweh is	| *gracious*	| *and compassionate*
---	| ***slow to anger***	| *and **rich in love***

Psalm 145:8

Sometimes words from the second line are repeated verbatim with a different emphasis added in the second (or more) line(s).

Ascribe to Yahweh	| *O mighty ones*
Ascribe to Yahweh	| ***glory and strength***
Ascribe to Yahweh	| ***the glory due His name***
Worship Yahweh	| ***in the splendor of His holiness***

Psalm 29:1-2

In the last line, we can see the equivalence of meaning between "ascribe [glory to] Yahweh" and "worship Yahweh." The terms "glory" and "splendor" are also parallel, yet "holiness" is a distinctive element. In such situations, the categories of synonymous parallelism and synthetic become blurred. Our chief interest, however, is not in giving labels, but in recognizing how parallelism works.

There are several other favorite devices in the biblical poets' "bag of tricks." These include the following:

Inclusio: Using the same line or phrase both at the beginning and end of a passage.

Praise Yahweh, O my soul . . . Praise Yahweh, O my soul.

Psalm 103

Chiasm: Like "inverted parallelism," similar thoughts are placed in mirror-image order.

```
A                          A                          A
  B                          B                          B
    C                          C                          C
  B                          A                          B
A                            B                            C
                               C                        A
```

A   *Unless Yahweh builds the house*
    B   *its builders labor in vain*
A   *Unless Yahweh watches over the city*
    B   *the watchmen stand in guard in vain*

Psalm 127:1

A   *May God be gracious to us and bless us make His face shine upon us*

   B   *May Your ways be known on earth*

      C   *May the peoples praise You, O God:*

        May all the peoples praise You

         D   *May the nations be glad and sing for joy*

           for You rule the people justly

           and guide the nations of the earth

      C   *May the peoples praise You, O God;*

        may all the peoples praise You

   B   *Then the land will yield its harvest,*

      And God, our God, will bless us

A   *God will bless us,*

   And all the ends of the earth will fear Him

Acrostics: An "alphabet" poem in which the first verse begins with the first letter of the alphabet, the second verse with the second letter, etc. Acrostic passages include Psalms 9-10; 25; 34; 37; 111; 112; 119; 145; Proverbs 31:10-31; Lamentations 1-4; and Nahum 1:2-10.

Figures of Speech: One of the chief features of all poetry in any language is figurative speech. These include simile, metaphor, personification, hyperbole, metonymy, merism, apostrophe, anthropomorphism, etc.

Word-pairs: Because biblical poetry operates by paralleling the lines, certain words become commonly linked. They are pairs which frequently appear in parallel lines of poetry. Some of these word pairs include *foes/enemies; Yahweh/God; nations/peoples; kings/rulers* (or *princes*); *thousand/ten-thousand; poor/oppressed;*

justice/righteousness; heavens/earth; silver/gold; sin/ transgression; wickedness/evil; way/path; wilderness/ desert; plan/purpose; sing/rejoice; instruct/teach; eyes/ ears; love (truth)/faithfulness; etc.

Some of these pairs appear together to indicate totality. The pair *day/night* means "all the time" (so does *[when I] sleep/ wake*); *heaven/earth* means "everywhere" (as does *near/ far*); *young/old* means "all people"; etc. This technique is actually a figure of speech called *merism*.

Interruptions: Poets use patterns of words to create symmetry, balance, and artistic appeal. Frequently in biblical poetry, however, an established pattern will "break form." Be especially alert when this happens, because the "odd" element is being emphasized. (This kind of thing is very noticeable in a chiasm pattern of A, B, C, D, C, B, A. The "D" part of the poem is the part where we are supposed to say, "ah ha!")

Form: The forms of the Psalms (praise, lament, thanksgiving, hymn) are standard "outlines" which govern their structure. These also may be altered for emphasis.

For Further Reflection:

THE ELEMENTS

At Westwinds Church we believe that being a Jesus follower requires movement. Doing something, engaging, shadowing God, and inviting Jesus into your everyday—becoming increasingly aware of how God is at work in the world around you.

This all sounds like good advice but sometimes we need a little help knowing where to start. If you hang around Westwinds, you are familiar with *The Elements*. They boil down to this: based on the teaching of the Bible, we encourage you to do something for your church, your world, your soul, and your relationships. These four areas are key areas that need attention for us to stretch our spiritual muscles—to do *something*.

Some call these exercises spiritual formation. Some call them spiritual disciplines. Others call them spiritual practices.

At Westwinds, we approach *The Elements* in seasons, for stints of time. We call them Waves. We encourage our whole church to participate in each Wave together. We have printed this Wave's options here for you.

They are suggestions. They are things we encourage you to try on for size. Some may not be for you. Others may be life changing. We encourage you to make up your own options as well.

All the suggestions below are the work of Becky Veydt. *The Elements* are under her care at Westwinds. If you have any questions regarding *The Elements*, please email becky.veydt@westwinds.org.

SOUL:

1. Sing a New Song (even if you think you can't sing)
Both Psalms 96 and 98 encourage the reader to "Sing to the Lord a new song." Consider how it is your life has been a song. If you were to live a new song, how would it be different from the old one? What would change? Take some time to think on and pray about this. Make a list and talk to God about how you desire for these changes to be part of the new song you would like to "sing" for Him. Commit to follow His leading in implementing these changes and believe that He will give you the strength to do so, because He will if you ask Him.

2. "Please Interrupt Me."
How has God's Spirit been interrupting your life? Are you aware that He is trying? Are you aware that He wants your permission and invitation to co-author your story? For the next week (or longer), begin each morning by inviting God to interrupt your day, to nudge you towards awareness of His presence in the mundane and normal everyday. Then observe how He actually acts, interrupts, nudges you. What kind of difference did it make in your day? In your spirit? Attitude? Awareness of others? Choice of actions? End each day by talking with God about your experience.

3. Write Your Own Psalm or Examine Psalm 99 (chapter 10)
Try your hand at poetry by writing your own Psalm following some of the structure and format suggestions found in chapter two of this atlas. Topically you may find the need to "complain, cry, gain perspective and then praise" or simply to make it a declaration of God's presence and work in your life. Whatever the outcome, simply make it honest. OR, if you prefer, take some time to study Psalm 99 and then answer the questions found in chapter ten. We suggest you journal as you do, writing down your observations, thoughts and discoveries.

4. Spirit and Truth

The Bible indicates that God is looking for people who worship Him in Spirit and in truth. What do you think that means? Do you worship Him in Spirit and Truth? Are you free in allowing God's Spirit to guide you? Are you seeking truth? If not, what do think holds you back? Ask God to help you discover what it means to be such a worshiper.

RELATIONSHIPS:

1. Permission, Encouragement, Freedom

Who in your life gave you permission, encouragement and freedom to become, experiment and discover? Make a list of these individuals and if possible thank them by writing each a note. While you're at it, tell God thanks for each person.

2. Catch 'Em in the Act

If you don't already do this, make a concerted effort to catch your children doing things worth praising and then, well, praise them for it. Try to say more positive things to your children in a given day then negative. It may take some time to get to this point, and there may be seasons, but stick with the practice.

3. Re-write a Psalm With Your Small Group or Family

Choose a Kingly Psalm to focus upon and spend some time as a group going over it line by line, discussing it as you go. What words jump out to you? What patterns, thoughts or ideas within the Psalm catch your attention? Anything you need to look up? Once your group has a good grasp of the Psalm, try re-wording it phrase by phrase to give it tangible, modern day meaning for your lives. Have someone write it down as you go.

4. Permission, Encouragement, Freedom (But the other side of the coin)

You have influence and opportunity to offer someone in your life, whether it be a child, relative, co-worker, friend, etc, the chance to experience permission and freedom to explore without risk. It may be an artistic endeavor, a vocational exploration, a spiritual conversation or something else. Who can you encourage in this way? How can you offer it? Make a concentrated effort to provide a safe environment for permission to be given, encouragement to be felt and freedom to be experienced.

CHURCH:

1. How Do You Prepare for Church?

Worship isn't something that simply happens when we walk into church. It is something we bring with us; a carryover from time spent with God during the week. Next time you go to church, examine the attitude you are taking with you. How do you prepare? What is your focus? Ask God to help you show up with a focus set upon Him. A good way to help set your own perspective is by remembering the many things God has done for you.

2. WE Christmas

At the point of this writing, it is currently late October and we are gearing up for the holidays at Westwinds. We have an ongoing practice of going to our local charities and asking them what they need and then from that, creating a wish list of items that would help them better care for the peoples they serve. If you go to the Winds, plan to participate in WE Christmas by purchasing an item off of the wish list and returning it back to the Winds on the designated date (contact info@westwinds.org to find out more).

If you are not at the Winds, we suggest you get together with a few others and do something similar at your church or organization this holiday season (for that matter, who needs a season? Organizations have needs all year long). You can usually find a list of service organizations in your area through your local chamber of commerce.

3. Invite Someone

One of the hallmarks of authentic Jesus Followers is that they are inviters. They are eager to share with others the good things they have experienced and invite them to discover it too. Why not invite someone to join you at Westwinds (or your church)? Better yet, why don't you bring them with you and share a meal either before or after? Try to do this at least once in the next month. Maybe even try it once a month with different people for the whole next year.

4. Are You Still at War?

We discussed earlier, in chapter nine, the war that has taken place within the Church over the concept of musical worship. What is your position? Are you still at war? If so, why? What have you gained and lost in this "dialogue"? How do the points shared within the chapter challenge your current thoughts? Talk to God about these areas.

WORLD:

1. Let the Music Play

Following the Psalmist's instruction for us to sing a new song, how can you breath new life into a place that is crying out for God's presence? It may be your workplace, your neighborhood, your local school or coffee shop.

What can you do to demonstrate God's tangible redemptive presence in the world? Pray, observe, brainstorm, keep praying, invite others to participate, initiate action, keep praying, follow through, respond humbly, praise God.

2. "Well I Declare..."

The Kingly Psalms are full of declarations about God; who He is, what He has done, how His presence makes a difference. They are stories of remembrance and stances of faith. How are you at making declarations? When is the last time you publicly declared God's presence in your life and shared how He has made a difference? Ask God to open a door for you to do so and then when He does, walk through it. Simply be faithful to share how God has touched your own personal life. No one can argue with that.

3. Canned

Many schools and organizations are stepping up to counter the ever-growing poverty problem we have in the US. Around Jackson, where Westwinds is located, we have school sponsored "weekend backpack programs" and organizational driven food drives. By contacting your local news paper or community action agency you can find out more about what is happening in your area. Once you find something worth giving to, we suggest you try making a giving plan. Rather than giving once, donate weekly. Try to donate at the same time, on the same day, at the same place. Let it become a habit in your life (and hopefully a modeled practice for others to observe and follow).

4. Room Around the Table

Chances are there is someone in your circle of contact (church, workplace, neighborhood, etc.) or maybe even several someones, (a family perhaps), that don't have a place to go this Thanksgiving (Easter, Fourth of July, New Years or just on Sunday). What about your house? There is nothing like having a meal with others to create friendships. Who could you invite to your table? Contact them this week and invite them over.

𝕽esources:

Read the Bible for a Change: Understanding and Responding to God's Word by Ray Lubeck

Reflections on the Psalms by C.S. Lewis

Commentary on the Psalms Volume 4 by John Calvin

Interpreting the Psalms: An Exegetical Handbook by Mark D. Futato and David M. Howard

The Exositor's Bible Commentary Volume 5: Psalms by Willem A. VanGemeren. Edited by Frank E. Gaebelein

Psalms: Reading and Studying the Book of Praises by W. H. Bellinger

Old Testament Theology by John H. Sailhamer

The Search for Christian America by Mark A. Noll, Nathan O. Hatch and George M. Marsden

Living Beyond the Daily Grind: Reflections on the Songs and Sayings of Scripture Book 1 & 2 by Charles R. Swindoll

The Book of Psalms: A Translation with Commentary by Robert Alter

The Bible Knowledge Commentary by John F. Walvoord and Roy B. Zuck

King Me

John Voelz

CPSIA information can be obtained at www.ICGtesting.com
Printed in the USA
BVOW03s2310160414

350666BV00001B/31/P

9 780982 612484